SUTTON POCKET HISTORIES

THE ANGLO-SAXONS

BARBARA YORKE

SUTTON PUBLISHING

First published in the United Kingdom in 1999 by
Sutton Publishing Limited · Phoenix Mill
Thrupp · Stroud · Gloucestershire · GL5 2BU

British Library Cataloguing in Publication Data
A catalogue record for this book is available from the British
Library.

ISBN 0-7509-2220-6

*Cover illustration: The Kingston Brooch, courtesy of the Board of Trustees
of the National Museums & Galleries on Merseyside (Liverpool Museum)*

™   ALAN SUTTON™ and SUTTON™ are the
trade marks of Sutton Publishing Limited

Typeset in 11/16 pt Baskerville.
Typesetting and origination by
Sutton Publishing Limited.
Printed in Great Britain by
The Guersey Press Company Limited,
Guernsey, Channel Islands.

Contents

For my parents,
Derek and Enid Troubridge, in their
Golden Wedding year

List of Dates

680	Death of Abbess Hild of Whitby.
685	Battle of Nechtansmere; King Ecgfrith of Northumbria slain by Picts.
687	Death of Bishop Cuthbert of Lindisfarne.
688	King Cadwalla of Wessex abdicates in order to be baptised in Rome; accession of Ine.
690	Death of Archbishop Theodore.
716	Accession of King Æthelbald of Mercia.
722	Boniface appointed bishop in Germany.
726	Death of King Ine of Wessex.
731/2	Bede completes *Ecclesiastical History of the English People*.
735	Death of Bede.
757	Murder of King Æthelbald of Mercia; accession of Offa.
768	Accession of Charlemagne, King of the Franks.
786	King Cynewulf of Wessex killed by Cyneheard; accession of Beorhtric.
787	Creation of archbishopric of Lichfield; Ecgfrith consecrated as King of Mercia.
793	Viking attack on Lindisfarne.
796	Deaths of Kings Offa and Ecgfrith of Mercia.
802	Accession of Ecgbert of Wessex.
814	Death of Charlemagne.
838	King Ecgbert defeats Cornish and their Viking allies.
860	Viking attack on Winchester.
866	Arrival of the 'Great Army'.
867	Great Army defeats Northumbrian kings.
869	King Edmund of East Angles killed by Great Army.
871	Death of King Æthelred of Wessex; accession of Alfred.

874	King Burgred of Mercia driven out by Great Army.
878	King Alfred defeats Guthrum at the battle of Edington.
886	King Alfred entrusts London to Æthelred of Mercia.
899	Death of King Alfred; accession of Edward the Elder.
910	Danes of York defeated by King Edward.
918	Death of Æthelflaed, Lady of the Mercians.
924	Death of King Edward; accession of Athelstan.
927	King Athelstan takes York.
937	King Athelstan victorious at battle of Brunanburh.
939	Death of King Athelstan; succession of Edmund.
946	Death of King Edmund; accession of Eadred.
954	Death of Eric Bloodaxe; submission of York to King Eadred.
955	Death of King Eadred; succession of Eadwig.
957	Edgar created King of Mercia.
959	Death of King Eadwig; Edgar becomes King of England; Dunstan appointed Archbishop of Canterbury.
961	Oswald appointed Bishop of Worcester.
963	Æthelwold appointed Bishop of Winchester.
973	Consecration of King Edgar at Bath; submission of Norse and Celtic kings at Chester.
975	Death of King Edgar; accession of Edward the Martyr.
978	Murder of King Edward; accession of Æthelred.
980	Resumption of Viking attacks.
984	Death of Bishop Æthelwold.

991	Battle of Maldon.
994	King Æthelred and Olaf Tryggvason in alliance.
1002	King Æthelred marries Emma of Normandy.
1007	Eadric Streona created Ealdorman of Mercia.
1012	King Æthelred institutes heregeld to pay for army of Thorkell the Tall.
1013	Submission of English to Swein of Denmark; King Æthelred in exile.
1014	Death of Swein; return of King Æthelred.
1016	Death of King Æthelred; succession and death of Edmund Ironside; Cnut becomes King of England.
1017	King Cnut marries Emma
1018	Cnut becomes King of Denmark; Godwine appointed Earl of Wessex
1035	Death of King Cnut; William becomes Duke of Normandy.
1037	Harold Harefoot recognised as King of England.
1040	Death of King Harold I; accession of Harthacnut.
1042	Death of King Harthacnut; accession of Edward the Confessor.
1051	Temporary exile of Earl Godwine and sons.
1057	Return and death of Edward the Exile.
1066	Death of King Edward the Confessor; accession of Harold Godwineson; defeat and death of Harald Hardrada and Tostig at Stamford Bridge; defeat and death of King Harold II at Hastings; Duke William crowned King of England.
1085	Domesday Book commissioned.

Map 1: The early Anglo-Saxon kingdoms, c. 650.

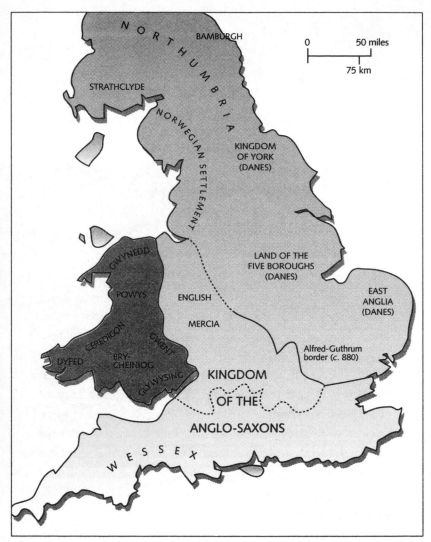

NORTHUMBRIA

BAMBURGH

STRATHCLYDE

NORWEGIAN SETTLEMENT

KINGDOM
OF YORK
(DANES)

0   50 miles

75 km

GWYNEDD

POWYS

ENGLISH

LAND OF THE
FIVE BOROUGHS
(DANES)

EAST
ANGLIA
(DANES)

CEREDIGION

GWENT

MERCIA

DYFED

BRY-
CHEINIOG

GLYWYSING

Alfred-Guthrum
border (c. 880)

KINGDOM

OF THE

ANGLO-SAXONS

W E S S E X

Map 2: England, c. 900

Introduction

Unlike some early medieval peoples, such as the Vikings, the Anglo-Saxons do not have a dominant image for people today. That is how it should be because the Anglo-Saxon period is a long one, stretching from the fifth to the eleventh centuries, and there were many changes within that time – the formation of kingdoms out of post-Roman chaos, the conversion to Christianity, Scandinavian settlement and the creation of a united kingdom of England under one dynasty. Anglo-Saxons were never a homogenous whole, but a stratified and multicultural society, so that one image could never stand for all.

There is reason for gratitude, therefore, that the name 'Anglo-Saxon' does not automatically conjure up images of horned helmets and burning ships, but the lack of a popular image has also meant that people living in England today are not always aware of their close links with an Anglo-Saxon past. The situation was very different in the nineteenth century when it was believed that features of the 'English character' – bravery, a sense of justice, a refusal to be cast down by adversity, an unquenchable desire to conquer new lands – were inherited from Germanic forebears. Such sentiments, sometimes bordering on nationalistic racism, may have served to discredit the Anglo-Saxon past, but they are ideas foisted on the period by later centuries. In the fifth to eleventh centuries, to be 'Anglo-Saxon' was not to be necessarily of Germanic descent, but an indication of political and cultural allegiance.

The legacy of the Anglo-Saxons is shared by anyone living in England today, and cannot be ignored because it is all around us. It includes not only tangible signs such as earthworks and churches, but also the language that we speak and the places in which we live. England as a geographical and political entity was the creation of the Anglo-Saxon past, and this book is intended to provide a guide to the main events and developments that attended its gestation.

ONE

The Arrival of the Anglo-Saxons

The fifth and sixth centuries are the most difficult periods of Anglo-Saxon history to study because of a shortage of written sources. The Anglo-Saxons did not become literate, apart from a few short runic inscriptions, until after their conversion to Christianity, which mostly occurred during the seventh century. In the eighth and ninth centuries the foundation traditions of some of the Anglo-Saxon royal houses were written down, but these display many features of Germanic-origin legends and should not be regarded as genuine records of what actually occurred. Nor should the dates attached to the accounts be trusted, because the Anglo-Saxons had no universal system of dating until after their conversion.

There are a few ambiguous references to events in Britain in documents from Continental Europe and

Byzantium, but the best guide to what happened during the fifth and sixth centuries is provided by the British cleric Gildas in his 'Ruin of Britain'. Exactly when and where this work was written are much debated, but many historians would date it to about AD 550 and place its composition in western Britain, perhaps Dorset or Somerset. Gildas was not aiming to write a history; as he says he employed 'lament rather than analysis'. What he produced was an extended sermon, through which he hoped to alert his fellow Britons to their failings as Christians. His account included a brief résumé of their history since they had been informed by the Roman authorities that they could no longer defend the province and that it was, in effect, no longer part of the Roman Empire. The severance of Britain from Rome is usually dated, with the aid of sources written on the Continent, to about 410. Gildas relates how the British leaders, being much troubled by attacks from the Picts of Scotland, decided to employ some of the Saxons, who had also been raiding British shores, as federate troups to protect eastern England from these attacks from the north.

All went well to begin with, but further settlers joined the Saxons until they were sufficiently numerous to win the initiative from their British hosts and seize power for themselves. A successful rallying of forces under Ambrosius Aurelianus (one of the few individuals mentioned by name by Gildas) prevented Saxon expansion further west, especially after the battle of Mount Badon, which had occurred in the year of Gildas's birth and is generally dated to about 500. This battle is attributed in later Celtic tradition to the largely mythical King Arthur. When Gildas wrote, the British kingdoms of the west were still independent of Saxon control or influence, though Gildas warned them that unless they improved their ways God might unleash the Saxon plague on them again.

The action of the British leaders in allowing the Saxons to settle may sound foolhardy, but by the fifth century there had been a long tradition of employing Germans in the Roman army and settling them in certain areas in return for military service. Items buried in some of the earliest Saxon cemeteries in Britain suggest that a number of the Saxon settlers had seen service in the Roman army. The location of some of these earliest burials in the vicinity of Roman towns in the east and in places like

Dorchester-on-Thames, well away from the coast but in strategically important positions, could support the idea of fighting forces settled by Roman authorities. However, it is hard to definitely provide confirmation for Gildas's explanation of the Saxon settlement in eastern England through archaeological evidence, and it may be that there is not just one explanation of how the Saxons came to Britain.

What is not in doubt is that there was migration from North Sea areas to Britain during the fifth century. In the additions which the great Anglo-Saxon historian Bede made to Gildas's account in his *Ecclesiastical History of the English People*, completed in about 731, he records that the bulk of the settlers came from three major Germanic groups, the Angles and Saxons of northern Germany, and the Jutes of Denmark; Gildas, like a number of contemporary writers, called all Continental Germans 'Saxons'. Archaeological evidence has broadly supported Bede's identifications, because burial practices (both inhumation and cremation), jewellery styles, weapons and house-types that are characteristic of these areas begin to appear in eastern Britain during the course of the fifth century. It has also been shown that sites in the North Sea homelands were deserted at this time, in apparent support of Bede's statement that parts had remained unoccupied into his day.

But archaeological finds and place-name evidence also suggest that Bede's statement was a simplification of a more complex picture and that settlers came from several other Germanic groups as well, including Franks, Frisians, Norwegians and Swabians, whose separate identities were subsequently subsumed in the identification of certain areas as Anglian, Saxon or Jutish. The names of the early Anglo-Saxon kingdoms (see Map 1) show that the east and north-east were considered as 'Anglian' areas, and the south was predominantly 'Saxon', apart from Kent, the Isle of Wight and southern Hampshire which Bede records as 'Jutish'. These separate provincial identities were marked in the sixth century by the adoption of different styles of female dress.

What is less certain is any estimate of the actual number of Germanic settlers who came to Britain. Gildas implies that the Saxons destroyed Romanised life and he waxes particularly eloquent on the destruction of towns: 'All the major towns were laid low by the repeated battering of enemy rams: laid low, too, all the inhabitants – church leaders, priests and people alike, as the swords glinted all around and the flames crackled. It was a sad sight. In the middle of the squares the foundation-stones of high walls and towers that had been torn from their lofty base, holy altars, fragments of corpses, covered (as it were) with the purple crust of congealed blood, looked as though they had been mixed up in some dreadful wine-press.'

Gildas's account was at one time taken to imply that overwhelming numbers of incoming Germans would have been necessary to overthrow Roman Britain, but we now know through archaeological studies that life in Britain had already begun to change significantly in the fourth century. Internal problems caused the collapse of many aspects of Romanisation, not the incoming Saxons, for the changes happened not only in eastern England, but also in the western areas which did not come under Saxon control until the seventh century. Town life declined because the economy which supported towns no longer existed. Excavations have not validated Gildas's sensational picture of Saxons wreaking destruction and instead suggest that many former towns would have been all but deserted by the time the settlers arrived.

Many place-name specialists still feel that the dominance achieved by the English language argues for large numbers of settlers, especially as in other areas of the former Roman Empire which came under German control – such as the Roman province of Gaul which became Francia – Latin continued as the main language. But the dominance of English may have been achieved gradually. Our place-names today may be of mainly English origin, but they do not all date from the fifth and sixth centuries. Because of settlement-shift a significant proportion of the place-names in existence in the settlement period have been lost. Further support for large numbers has been taken from the way in which the material culture of the settlers had become dominant by the sixth century. However, one should be aware that, with the loss of access to Roman markets and with burial customs that did not necessarily include provision of grave goods, the British would have been less 'visible' in the archaeological record than the newcomers – excavated sites in the 'free' British areas of the west have shown that they characteristically have few finds and that many of these are not particularly distinctive. The argument is currently gaining ground that very large numbers would not have been necessary to bring about major changes in language and culture; the fact that the Anglo-Saxons were the providers of military power, and so became politically dominant, may be sufficient to explain the dominance of their language and culture without recourse to ethnic cleansing.

A key issue, therefore, is the relationship between the British living in eastern England and the incoming Germans. Gildas loathed Anglo-Saxons and frequently describes them as akin to wild beasts. He implies that there was little British survival in eastern England – the unfortunate Britons had either been slain by the Anglo-Saxons, enslaved or forced into exile. No doubt some of them were, but such wholesale destruction of the population would not have been necessary. With the relaxation of imperial control, there was enough spare land for both settlers and indigenous Britons. Furthermore, it is not what happened in the seventh century when written sources exist to show something of what occurred when Anglo-Saxons took control of areas of western Britain. A West Saxon lawcode of the late seventh century shows that British inhabitants of different ranks were living in the West Saxon kingdom with recognised legal rights. However, Britons were not as highly regarded or as well protected as Anglo-Saxons of the equivalent class so it is not surprising to find in the next surviving West Saxon lawcode of some two centuries later that the apartheid has disappeared – all the inhabitants of ninth-century Wessex regarded themselves as 'Anglo-Saxon'. The British had not been eliminated, they simply adopted the language and customs of the Anglo-Saxons who controlled the province, as it was in their obvious interest so to do.

Many archaeologists feel that such acculturation also occurred in eastern England in the sixth and seventh centuries. Many of those buried with Anglo-Saxon objects, or living in settlements where they were made and used, may not have been lineal descendants of Germanic migrants, but people of British descent who had adopted some of the attributes of what had become the dominant cultural group. Studies of burial customs, of variations in the height of skeletons and in the shape of feet seem to provide some support for the idea that a number of those buried in Anglo-Saxon cemeteries were of British origin, and ultimately it may be possible to prove (or disprove) the hypothesis through further scientific analysis of skeletal remains, though distinctions between incomers and natives would gradually have been eroded by intermarriage.

One striking example of apparent interaction between British and Anglo-Saxons is provided by the West Saxon royal house which purported to be of Germanic origin and descended from Woden, but had a founder with a British name (Cerdic) and several other princes whose names were either partly or purely Celtic. Other indicators of British survival and interaction with the newcomers come through place-names. Most areas of eastern England can provide some examples of survival, or partial Anglicisation, of Celtic and Latin place-names Nevertheless, it is likely that there were regional differences in the scale of Anglo-Saxon settlement. There appears to have been more concentrated migration into the Anglian areas of eastern England, where large cremation cemeteries are known, than into the Saxon areas of the south.

Various aspects of the fifth- and sixth-century Anglo-Saxon communities can be elucidated through archaeological studies. Typically they seem to have lived in extended households in small dispersed hamlets, and were predominantly concerned with subsistence farming. Life was frequently hard and closer to that of Third World countries today. There was high infant mortality, and skeletal analysis suggests that many people suffered periods of starvation or at least did not get adequate nutrition. The proportion of the population living to beyond sixty seems to have been small. Many skeletons show signs of lives involving hard physical labour and osteo-arthritic conditions. Germanic culture may have become dominant, but it would appear that many descendants of the original settlers had not greatly improved their lot by crossing the North Sea.

However, without written records there are always going to be major gaps of knowledge. Although it is recognised that before the advent of Christianity the Germanic peoples worshipped a variety of gods, very little is known of the details of their beliefs or rituals. Symbols on jewellery or pottery may refer to their gods or significant myths, but the key to their meaning is lost, unless links can be made with Scandinavian mythology which was recorded much later. Above all little can be learnt of politics and events. The sixth century can seem a period of relative peace and equality compared to the seventh century, but that perception may well be illusory because no records exist of the battles and feuds which dominate the earliest written accounts. Frankish sources suggest that 'Saxon' pirates were a major menace in the Channel in the sixth century, and some of these Viking-type groups may have been based in southern England and no doubt preyed on their countrymen as well as the Franks. Concern with controlling these groups may have led to some Frankish intervention in England, and there are hints of some form of Frankish overlordship of parts of England in their sources.

It is not even certain how eastern Britain was organised at this time, and whether there were rulers being supported by the rural communities as there were in Gildas's western Britain. Some archaeologists have argued for a complete 'systems collapse' when Britain ceased to be part of the Roman Empire, so that in the fifth and sixth centuries local groups were largely responsible for their own affairs, with elite groups emerging only gradually. On the other hand, there are some indications of survival of Roman boundaries and adminstrative areas. The names of Bernicia, Deira,

Kent and Lindsey – four of the earliest Anglo-Saxon kingdoms – are derived from those of Romano-British tribes or districts, and may have had their own native rulers before coming under Anglo-Saxon control. The kingdom of Elmet in West Yorkshire is a well-attested example of a British kingdom in the eastern half of the country which survived into the seventh century, and there may have been others. But the political history of much of the sixth century is lost, and it is not until near the end of the century that there were clearly Anglo-Saxon kingdoms in eastern England.

TWO

The Anglo-Saxon Kingdoms

As soon as a regular supply of written sources is forthcoming in the seventh century, content is dominated by kings and their activities. Bede, writing in 731, identifies some thirteen provinces which he would describe as kingdoms, and these are shown on Map 1. However, the situation in the seventh century is likely to have been fluid and there may once have been more kingdoms and a considerable fluctuation of boundaries. Some smaller units may have had their own independent rulers before being subsumed into one of the larger kingdoms. One example is a group called the Gyrwe who were based in the fens around Peterborough and Ely; Bede records a ruler of the South Gyrwe called Tondbert, who married a princess of the East Angles, and shortly after this union the province seems to have been incorporated into the East Anglian kingdom. Bede calls Tondbert a *princeps* (prince or leading man), but he may well have been regarded as a king by his own people. On the other hand, other short-lived kingdoms might have resulted from newly conquered territories being temporarily grouped together for administrative reasons. One such seems to have been the so-called 'kingdom of Surrey' (in fact incorporating a much larger area of southern England) which King Wulfhere created for his kinsman Frithuric through his conquests in southern England in the last quarter of the seventh century. Few of these gains became permanent annexations and the kingdom of Surrey soon disappeared again as its different component parts went their separate ways.

The earliest Anglo-Saxon kingdoms to become established were based in the south and east – not surprsingly in view of the pattern of Anglo-Saxon settlement. Bede has a list of dominant kings, and the earliest entries are Ælle of the South Saxons, Ceawlin of Wessex (d. 593), Æthelbert of Kent (d. 616) and Raedwald of the East Angles (d. *c.* 625); Ælle is said to have landed in Sussex in 477, but the fifth-century dates of the *Anglo-Saxon Chronicle* owe more to imagination than fact, and he is likely to have been closer in date to the time of Ceawlin of Wessex who follows him in the list. The kingdoms of the East Angles, Kent, the South Saxons and the West Saxons (at this time based in the Thames valley) all seem to have been established by the end of the sixth century, and to these probably should be added the East Saxons, whose royal house is known to have been in existence in 601. As discussed in Chapter One, it is possible that Anglo-Saxon rulers took over provinces previously under British control based on units of Roman local government (*civitates*) which could have provided them with some administrative infrastructure.

Coastal locations would have allowed continued contact with Germanic homelands, but also opportunities for piratical raiding which may have been a significant component in the early development of Anglo-Saxon kingship. The nearest Continental neighbours were the Franks who, perhaps because of a desire to control raiding in the Channel, seem to have interested themselves in south-east England in the sixth century. Æthelbert of Kent married a Frankish princess in about 580, and there are also hints of Frankish links for the royal houses of the East Angles and the East Saxons. Luxury goods produced in Francia, or imported via Francia from the Mediterranean, seem to have been status symbols at the south-eastern royal courts. The famous East Anglian ship burial at Sutton Hoo, which many think could have been the grave of King Raedwald, included several items of Byzantine silverware which may have reached East Anglia via Francia, perhaps as diplomatic gifts; the assemblage also included a purse of coins from Frankish mints. Trade with Francia, and other areas bordering the North Sea, may have become a significant element in the economy of these provinces by the end of the sixth century. The kings of Kent, in particular, seem to have benefited from their close proximity to the Frankish kingdom, and there seems to have been movement not only of people and commodities, but also of ideas. Kent was the first of the Anglo-Saxon kingdoms to be converted to Christianity, at the end of the sixth century, and the first to produce its own currency, modelled on that of Francia. Æthelbert of Kent produced the earliest surviving Anglo-Saxon lawcode, and it reveals a certain indebtedness to Frankish models. Kent had the advantage of controlling the shortest crossings to France, not only from Kent itself, but also from the Solent region whose rulers seem to have been in alliance with them and also claimed to be of Jutish descent.

After Raedwald, the next three most powerful kings in Bede's list – Edwin (616–33), Oswald (634–42) and Oswiu (642–70) – are all from Northumbria, Bede's home province. Northumbria was formed from the amalgamation of two kingdoms: Deira (between the Humber and the Tyne), and Bernicia (north of the Tyne) whose royal houses struggled for ascendancy over each other during the first half of the seventh century. In spite of Edwin of Deira's success in sending his Bernician rivals into exile, the Bernicians were ultimately triumphant and the last Deiran king was dispatched through the machinations of King Oswiu of Northumbria in 651. Also increasingly powerful in the latter part of the seventh century was the midland kingdom of Mercia which grew rapidly under the energetic leadership of Penda (d. 655) and his son Wulfhere (658–675). Northumbria and Mercia were able to establish an advantage over the south-eastern kingdoms because of their geographical positions which enabled them to quickly expand their territory through incorporation of British kingdoms to the west and north. The West Saxons realised where the advantage lay, and in the course of the seventh century shifted their centre of interest from the Thames valley to further south, which gave them the potential of expansion into the south-west.

The larger Anglo-Saxon kingdoms were able to absorb the smaller British kingdoms, or, as Mercia seems to have done on its western flank, to set up semi-independent satellite provinces such as those of the Hwicce and the Magonsaetan. But some Celtic kingdoms were expanding in a similar way, and the kingdoms of Powys and Gwynedd in Wales and that of the Picts in Scotland were more than a match for even the most ambitious Anglo-Saxon kingdoms. Sometimes British and Anglo-Saxon kingdoms acted in alliance. Penda of Mercia and Cadwallon of Gwynedd were jointly very successful in counteracting the growing power of Northumbria in the first half of the seventh century, and defeated and killed King Edwin and two of his successors in battle. The Northumbrians also found the Picts to their north to be formidable opponents and suffered a particularly calamitous defeat in 685 when

King Ecgfrith (son of Oswiu) and most of his army were killed after being trapped in a mountain pass at Nechtansmere (near Forfar in Angus). The disaster put an end to further Northumbrian expansion.

Military strength was the basis of royal power and so the kingdoms which could expand westwards ultimately had the advantage because they had the resources to field much larger armies than the kingdoms of the south-east. The powerful kings on Bede's list were military overlords who used their might to defeat or intimidate lesser rulers into paying them tribute. Sometimes the term 'bretwalda' is applied to them by modern historians, but, although the term is found once in the *Anglo-Saxon Chronicle*, it does not seem to have been regularly used by the Anglo-Saxons themselves. Kings, therefore, spent a lot of their recorded time fighting, either trying to impose overlordship or to resist it, with attack being the favoured form of defence. Consequently the relationship of a king with his armed following, or *comitatus*, was of the greatest importance. A somewhat idealised picture is provided in the famous Old English poem *Beowulf* which stresses the importance of unstinting loyalty from follower to leader and of protecting one's reputation above all else. But the poem also makes clear the economics which lay behind the heroic ideal. The warriors were entirely supported by their leaders who provided bed and board while they were on active service, and land on which to settle when they retired. The *comitatus* also expected rewards of status goods as part of their share of any victory, hence the poetic epithet 'lord of the rings' for a ruler.

This was a society where conspicuous display of the right equipment was all-important, and royal service was one of the main ways in which such items could be obtained. Seventh-century kings were in danger of being locked into a vicious circle of military activity; they needed their armies to maintain their position and needed to fight to give those armies something to do and to acquire via tribute the rewards they expected. As Bede observed, fighting men who were not sufficiently employed might drift away to find more active employment in a rival kingdom.

Kings were not entirely dependent on tribute for their support. An increasingly important resource was that provided by the populace they claimed to govern. In return for the 'protection' afforded by their kings, the ordinary farming inhabitants had to render regular payments of agricultural produce (*feorm*) to their local royal centres. For these purposes, and for the collection of tribute, the countryside was divided into taxable units called hides, in theory the amount of land necessary to support one household. Sometimes kings and their entourages moved between the royal centres, literally eating their way around the kingdom. However, if the army was on campaign, lesser subjects might be required to bring the food to them. Bede has a revealing story of Imma, a member of the Northumbrian *comitatus*, who was captured after a battle in 679 and hoped to avoid detection by pretending to be one of the peasants who had transported supplies to the army.

Military success may have enabled royal houses to establish themselves and to live relatively luxuriously, but might not in itself have ensured their continuation in leaner times. Having clawed their way to power, the founders of royal dynasties did not want to be overturned by the next successful military commander. They looked to strengthen their positions by drawing upon traditional attributes of Germanic kingship which included descent from the gods. The majority of royal houses for which genealogies survive claimed descent from Woden, the Germanic god of war – their military victories could be taken as a sign of his support. The East Saxons claimed descent from Seaxneat who is recorded as a leading deity of the Continental Saxons (also known as the 'Old Saxons'). Most genealogies also include other deities and Germanic heroes in their upper registers, and their claims tended to become more extravagant over time as the dynasties competed to have the most impressive ancestry.

Royal houses who successfully established their descent from the gods were able to draw on the belief that only those descended from the founder of the line were eligible for the throne. Unfortunately after a few generations that meant a considerable pool of potential candidates and many kingdoms of the seventh century were subject to coups by individuals who might be only distantly related to the previous king. Such individuals may already have had some experience of royal power and be controlling a subdivision of the main kingdom, but they usually depended on armed force to bring them to the throne. When Cadwalla was exiled from Wessex as a troublesome prince in 685 he got together an army and killed the king of the neighbouring province of the South Saxons. He was soon ousted from that kingdom, but the reputation he had established was sufficient to enable him to return to Wessex and take the throne. The older-established kingdoms of the south-east often had more stable royal houses where remote relatives lost their kingworthiness, but the often violent coups in the expanding kingdoms had the advantage of ensuring that a sufficiently ruthless individual, who could see off foreign enemies as well as his own kinsmen, was selected.

The necessities of war meant that minorities and the rule of women were not usual. The reign of only one woman appears in any of the early regnal lists, that of Seaxburh of Wessex, and she only ruled for a year, probably attempting to safeguard the kingdom for a son. Women generally seem to have been regarded as ineligible for the throne, but – Anglo-Saxon rulers being above all pragmatic – they could when convenient be seen as passing a right to rule to their heirs. When the royal house of Bernicia wished to take over the neighbouring kingdom of Deira, their ambitions were helped by the marriages of

Bernician rulers to Deiran princesses which enabled offspring to claim descent from both houses.

Descent from the gods also created a bond between people and ruler for it is likely that the kings participated in religious ceremonies which would ensure the essential support from the gods throughout the year. Another traditional attribute of kingship which was of value to their subjects was as enforcers of the law. There are four Kentish lawcodes surviving from the seventh century, and one West Saxon. Much Germanic law was self-regulatory in that the victims of crime and their relatives sought redress from the aggressor and his kin. But there was a role for kings in protecting those who did not have any kin, and in intervening if traditional methods did not seem to be working, or threatened internal peace. As kings were entitled to part of the fines if their intervention was necessary, they had a natural incentive to involve themselves in law. But they seem also to have appreciated that the promulgation of law provided an opportunity to increase control over society in ways advantageous to themselves.

Traditional Anglo-Saxon poems such as *Beowulf* give a rather rose-tinted view of the heroic world of

Anglo-Saxon kings. The view is dimly echoed in Bede's history which utilised stories couched in this tradition. However, a far less romantic judgement is provided by Gildas, whose British kings lived lives not dissimilar to those of their Anglo-Saxon counterparts; the 'privatisation' of military power gave rise to basically similar regimes in many parts of the former Roman Empire. Gildas bluntly denounced his rulers as corrupt tyrants whose military companions were 'bloody, proud and murderous men, adulterers and enemies of God'. From a twentieth-century perspective, and siding with Gildas, many facets of early medieval kingship would no doubt be considered morally unacceptable. His perspective, of course, was formed by his Christianity – the religion which was to bring more than religious change to the Anglo-Saxon world.

THREE

Conversion to Christianity

The conversion of the Anglo-Saxons to Christianity is a topic that is relatively well-covered in surviving written sources, not least because it was a particular concern of the major source for the seventh and early eighth centuries, *The Ecclesiastical History of the English People* by Bede. To Bede the most significant event on the way to the Anglo-Saxons becoming a fully Christianised people was the dispatch of a mission by Pope Gregory the Great which arrived in Kent in 597. King Æthelbert of Kent was already acquainted with Christianity as he had married a Christian Frankish wife who had arrived with Bishop Liudhard as her chaplain. Although it may have been Liudhard who began the work of conversion, Pope Gregory had heard that Æthelbert was not receiving all the help that he expected from Frankia and saw here an opportunity for intervention in order to bring back a former area of the Roman Empire to the Christian church. It is possible that Gregory had been interested in the prospect of converting the English for some time. Both Bede and the *Life of Pope Gregory*, written at the Northumbrian monastery of Whitby in the late seventh century, record that Gregory had once hoped to go on a mission to England himself after seeing English slave boys for sale in Rome: 'not Angles, but angels of God' he is said to have predicted after learning their nationality. Æthelbert agreed to accept baptism from Augustine, who led the mission, and soon afterwards Pope Gregory was writing to the Bishop of Alexandria boasting that through his agency ten thousand Anglo-Saxons had been converted – perhaps a rather overenthusiastic estimate.

Through Æthelbert's family connections and powers of persuasion as overlord, missionaries were introduced into the kingdoms of the East Saxons and the East Angles. King Saebert of the East Saxons was Æthelbert's nephew and was persuaded to establish a bishopric in London which Gregory at this stage intended as the archiepiscopal centre for southern England, but in East Anglia King Raedwald would only agree to add a Christian altar to his pagan temple. Even these modest beginnings were threatened with dissolution on the death of Æthelbert. The missionaries were expelled from London, and only a timely miracle prevented their expulsion from Kent after a difference of opinion over whether Æthelbert's son and successor, Eadbald, could marry his stepmother. The loss of London meant that the archbishopric remained at Canterbury, where Augustine had established his see, and, of course, it is still based there today. When Edwin of Northumbria wished to marry Eadbald's sister, the Canterbury mission was able to found its intended northern centre at York – though that too ran into difficulties on Edwin's death.

Many of the Anglo-Saxon kings were persuaded to accept Christianity through contacts with neighbouring peoples rather than by Pope Gregory's mission. In the south of England, the Franks were particularly influential, and it was his Frankish marriage which had first inclined Æthelbert towards Christianity. East Anglia was finally brought into the Christian fold when Sigebert, a son of Raedwald, returned from exile in Francia in about 630. He had a better appreciation of Christianity from having lived in a Christian country for several years and sought to introduce the type of religious institutions he had seen there, with the aid of his Frankish bishop Felix. Franks were also influential among the West Saxons. Their first missionary, Birinus, may have been a Frank, and much of the work of consolidating Christianity in Wessex was done by the Franks Agilbert and his nephew Leuthere as bishops of the West Saxons. Agilbert subsequently became Bishop of Paris.

Irish missionaries were also extremely influential. During the reign of Edwin of Northumbria, the Bernician princes Oswald and Oswiu went into exile in Ireland and became Christians. When he became King of Northumbria in 634, Oswald sent for a mission from the monastery of Iona, the foundation of St Columba based in an Irish colony in western Scotland, and established a see at Lindisfarne. Through the influence of Oswald and his brother Oswiu, who were both powerful overlords, missionaries from Lindisfarne went to work in other areas of England, including the provinces of the East Saxons and Mercia. But Irish influence stretched further than this. Many of the Franks who came to work in England, including Felix and Agilbert, were followers of a charismatic Irishman called Columbanus who established, or inspired, the foundation of a number of monasteries in northern Francia and Burgundy in the late sixth and early seventh centuries.

Nor should the fact be overlooked that in the course of the seventh century many Anglo-Saxons were coming into contact with British Christians as their political power spread westwards. Pockets of Christian worship may have survived in some areas of eastern England such as St Albans, but we know from Gildas that it was certainly flourishing in the west of the country. Gildas made some terrible accusations against his contemporaries, but he never accused them of following any religion except Christianity. Bede was extremely hostile to the British church and claimed that it had made no attempt to convert the Anglo-Saxons. But his Northumbrian perspective may not hold true for the whole of the country. Bede himself records British bishops of the west cooperating with a West Saxon bishop, and archaeologists in particular have become increasingly convinced that many Anglo-Saxons who moved into former British kingdoms simply adopted the religion of the majority of the population in the areas in which they settled.

Although Christianity was becoming widespread in England by about 660, there was no overarching organisation and many variations in custom. The basic tenets of Christianity were the same for Italian, Frankish, Irish and British Christians, but they might vary over such practices as the form of ordination for priests and the shape of tonsures. One bone of contention, which particularly exercised Bede and caused many practical problems, was the calculation of Easter. Various differing calendars which provided the date were produced in the sixth and seventh centuries, and some British and Irish churches were reluctant to abandon the one approved by their founders for that which became current in Rome. But as the Pope in Rome possessed the greater authority as the successor of the apostles of Peter and Paul, the papal calendar increasingly gained ascendancy. Such considerations certainly seem to have influenced King Oswiu when, at a synod held in the monastery of Whitby in 664 at which the calculation of Easter was debated, he ruled that in future the church of Northumbria would recognise the authority of Canterbury, and thus of Rome, rather than Iona.

Oswiu's decision at Whitby was an important stage in the unification of the Anglo-Saxon church, but the trend was brought to fruition during the archi-episcopate of Theodore of Tarsus (669–90). Theodore must rank as one of the most remarkable and distinguished men to serve as Archbishop of Canterbury. He was by training a Greek monk and considerable biblical scholar, who, although well into his sixties, was persuaded to take the appointment of archbishop by the Pope after the Anglo-Saxon candidate had unfortunately died of plague in Rome. He was, as Bede acknowledged, the first archbishop whom all the churches of England recognised. Theodore initiated the holding of regular councils (synods) of all the English bishops which were vital for establishing uniformity within the English church. He also increased the number of Anglo-Saxon bishoprics, for previously most kingdoms had only had one which was not sufficient to provide adequate pastoral care. With the aid of a North African abbot, Hadrian, who had travelled to England with him, Theodore established a school at Canterbury which trained many of the next generation of Anglo-Saxon churchmen and provided some of the best education available in western Europe.

Bede makes it appear that the conversion of the Anglo-Saxons to Christianity was a foregone conclusion once Augustine had set foot in England, but the Anglo-Saxon rulers were in fact reluctant to completely abandon the worship of the old gods which was intimately linked with the Germanic concept of kingship. Individual rulers may have been converted to Christianity but rarely, to begin with, all the males of the royal houses so that Christian kings were often followed by pagan successors. This happened on more than one occasion among the East and West Saxons; the first West Saxon king was converted in 635, but it was still possible for Cadwalla to come to the throne in 685 unbaptised. Yet the conversion of the royal houses was essential if a wider conversion was to be achieved. Augustine could make little headway in Kent until he had baptised Æthelbert – something presumably indicative of the role of kings in pre-Christian religion. Only the kings could provide the church with the protection it needed, which was the main reason for the writing down of Æthelbert's lawcode. Kings also had to provide land and support for the building of churches, and written charters were introduced in the course of the seventh century to safeguard these grants.

Christianity ultimately prevailed because it had much to offer kings. The idea of the king as God's representative on earth compensated for the loss of direct descent from the pagan gods (though these were retained in genealogies, but reinterpreted as ordinary humans). The Christian God could be promoted as a successful winner of battles for his adherents, and Bede particularly stresses this aspect. The teaching that people should obey their ruler as they would obey God must also have been very attractive to rulers. Christianity had the further advantage of association with the Roman Empire, and with dominant and successful Germanic groups in western Europe such as the Franks. Of course, Bede would argue that it was the religious message that was ultimately most significant, and the answers it provided to the troublesome question of what happened after death may have been especially attractive. After an intitial reluctance to fully embrace Christianity, many new royal converts were prepared to abandon royal office for the sake of the new religion. Sigebert of the East Angles spent most of his reign in a monastery, and Cadwalla of Wessex resigned his throne after only three years as king in order to travel to Rome to be baptised. Churchmen seem to have been concerned to curb this type of enthusiasm. The last thing they wanted was Gildas's experience of a king who became an abbot and murdered two of his kinsmen in his church. As Bede observed, being a king and being a bishop required quite different personalities and priorities. The church was happier with the idea of women of the royal house entering into its service, and many of the earliest and most significant monasteries, such as Whitby, were run by abbesses of royal descent.

If it took the best part of the seventh century to fully introduce the royal houses to Christianity one can imagine that the conversion of ordinary folk was an even longer process. There were few bishops to begin with and only in the last quarter of the seventh century were many minster churches – monasteries, or other foundations with a body of priests – established. Some provinces seem to have had a fairly regular provision of such churches, perhaps with a minster church founded in each major administrative subdivision (*regio*) of the kingdom. In others provision may have been more haphazard, and there may have been variations in any case in the degree of interest taken in pastoral care. Bede was concerned that some settlements were lucky to see a priest once a year. But the move to Christianity would have been helped by the fact that the major festivals of the Christian calendar already conformed to the pattern of the agricultural year in the west and so would have coincided with pagan festivities. When Pope Gregory realised that England was less Romanised than he had originally thought, he urged his missionaries to make the most of such coincidences and to find bridges between the two religions, even to the extent of converting temples into churches. The recognition from the late seventh century of native saints, often with links to local churches or traditional holy sites such as wells, would also have made acceptance of Christianity easier. Saints were generally leading churchmen, like Bishop Cuthbert of Lindisfarne, or members of royal houses, such as King Oswald of Northumbria, who died fighting the pagan Penda. Many people may not have realised to begin with how much Christianity differed from their previous experiences of religion. The adoption of Old English words such as *halig* (holy), which might already have religious and social connotations, may have helped the transition, but could also have led to some confusions. The application of the word 'lord', previously used for the leader of a *comitatus*, seems to have led to the idea that Christ went around with a warband of apostles.

By 700 significant achievements had been made. England had some monasteries which could rival any of those found in Europe. Among the most outstanding was the dual foundation of Wearmouth and Jarrow, where Bede spent his life from the age of seven. Their founder, a Northumbrian nobleman called Benedict Biscop, travelled several times to Rome to acquire fittings and manuscripts for his churches. He was able to assemble an impressive library which fuelled the scholarship of Bede. Although he is remembered today chiefly as a historian, Bede's main writings were biblical commentaries and he was regarded as a leading theologian throughout the Middle Ages. Parts of the churches of Wearmouth and Jarrow still stand. Such churches were the first stone buildings to be built in England since the Roman period. Bede made mention that Benedict imported masons from Francia, and also glaziers; remnants of the stained glass they produced have been found in excavation. Such artefacts are a reminder that with the adoption of Christianity, the Anglo-Saxons were not only reconnecting with the religion and culture of the late Roman world, but also were reacquiring some of its technology as well. Other introductions by the church were to bring about wider social changes, but these became more apparent in the following century.

FOUR

Mercian Dominance

The political situation in the eighth century was dominated by two powerful Mercian kings, Æthelbald (716–57) and his cousin Offa (757–96). After reviewing the holders of bishoprics in the southern province of England in 731, Bede remarked that 'all these kingdoms and the other southern kingdoms which reach up to the Humber, together with their various kings, are subject to Æthelbald, king of the Mercians'. His terminology implies that he was ranking Æthelbald alongside the great overlord kings of the seventh century. Æthelbald's own perception of his superiority over other contemporary rulers is implied in some of his charter titles. 'King of the South English' was one of the forms with which he experimented, and he even witnessed one grant as *rex Britanniae*, 'king of Britain'. But although Æthelbald may have dominated his contemporaries, when he was murdered in 757 his eventual successor Offa had to begin building up an equivalent power base all over again. Offa seems to have appreciated the weaknesses of the traditional overlordship system and aimed to create something more long-lasting. He preferred to call himself *rex Merciorum,* 'king of the Mercians', and to concentrate on extending the borders of Mercia by incorporating previously independent kingdoms.

In some ways Offa's policy was an accelerated expansion of what Mercia had been doing very successfully since the seventh century. Penda and his sons had already incorporated the eastern provinces of Lindsey and the Middle Saxons into Mercian territory. Offa extended the process on a greater scale by redefining the status of subject kings in relationship to himself. The stages can be traced in charters by which the rulers of the Hwicce and the South Saxons, whose province Offa invaded in 771, were redesignated first as subkings and then as ealdormen – officials who governed a province on behalf of a king, but were not of regal status themselves (even though some might be of royal descent). The final stage was the apparent disappearance of the native dynasties altogether and their replacement by other ealdormen who were presumably Offa's own nominees. The same fate seems to have overtaken the royal house of the Magonsaetan.

The rulers of Kent and the East Angles put up a more determined stand. Offa first intervened in Kent in 764 and began to restrict the independence of the Kentish kings, spurring them to a temporarily successful resistance in 776. By 785 Offa was in control once again. A prince of the royal house, Eadbert Praen took refuge in Francia and endeavoured to win back the kingdom on the death of Offa, but was defeated by his successor Coenwulf; that is the last heard of the native dynasty. Mercian encroachment on East Anglia may have begun in the reign of Æthelbald if a King Beonna, who divided the kingdom with a native ruler in 749, has been correctly equated with Beornred, a Mercian of likely royal descent who briefly took the throne on Æthelbald's death before he was deposed by Offa. The East Anglian royal house probably regained control at that point, but in the 790s Offa was minting coins in his own name in the province and seems to have arranged the murder of its king Æthelbert in 794.

But if the East Anglian kings were down, they were not out, and in the ninth century they had the satisfaction of defeating and killing two Mercian kings in battle.

However, not all the remaining royal houses of Anglo-Saxon England were subjected to this type of treatment. The East Saxon dynasty continued to rule, although they seem to have been obliged to surrender London and its dependent area to Æthelbald. The West Saxons, though, with their much larger territory, were never seriously at risk of Mercian dominance, even if there was fighting between the two kingdoms over control of the Thames valley. Wessex and Mercia may have been in alliance towards the end of Offa's reign when King Beorhtric married Offa's daughter, Eadburh, albeit she left behind her a reputation, according to King Alfred, for tyrannical and arrogant behaviour – perhaps a projection of her father's attributes. King Æthelred I of Northumbria also married one of Offa's daughters, but relations between the kingdoms seems to have remained at that diplomatic level.

One disadvantage which both Wessex and Northumbria had in the eighth century, in contrast to Mercia, was much greater internal disturbance caused by disputes over the throne between rival branches of the royal houses. In 786, for instance, the reign of King Cynewulf was ended by an attempted coup by Cyneheard, the brother of the man Cynewulf had deposed in order to become king some twenty-nine years before; both Cynewulf and Cyneheard were killed during the incident. Ambition and revenge also loomed large in Northumbrian internal politics. King Æthelred, who was deposed in 779 in favour of King Ælfwold, had his revenge when he returned for a second reign in 790 and in the following years lured the two sons of Ælfwold from sanctuary and had them murdered. Mercia was not entirely free of such troubles; Æthelbald is said to have been murdered by his own *comitatus*, leading to a violent competition for the throne between Beornred and Offa. Offa is reputed to have had a number of kinsmen put to death to try to ensure the succession of his son. But the relative stability of two long reigns must have helped the concentration of resources on the expansion of Mercian power. However, in the ninth century Mercia was to experience the same type of rivalry between competing royal branch lines which bedevilled Northumbria and Wessex in the eighth.

Among the problems with which rulers of the eighth century had to contend were those caused by the introduction of new concepts of land law in the seventh century to meet the needs of the church. It would appear that before this point a king had made grants of land to his followers for their lifetimes only, but that did not suit the church which needed grants in perpetuity. Such permanent grants of land were known as 'bookland' as they were guaranteed by a *boc*, that is, a charter. After the concept had been established, lay nobles began to desire permanent grants of land too and, according to Bede, set up pseudo-monasteries to get these advantages and others associated with bookland, such as freedom from military service. In the early eighth century, Bede told his correspondent Bishop Egbert of York that a major cause of Northumbria's problems was stocks of royal land being so seriously depleted that the kings could no longer raise adequate armies.

The Mercian kings' solution to the problems was to claim that rulers retained certain inherent rights over land which had been granted out. The church naturally objected and complained of violations by royal officials, but a compromise appears to have been reached in which certain 'common burdens' – service in the army, the building of fortresses and the maintenance of roads and bridges – were recognised as obligatory on the whole realm with no possibility of exemption. Such rights may have enabled Offa to build the famous earthen dyke which bears his name on the frontier between Mercia and Powys. Some of the earliest known fortified centres (burhs) may also date to his reign; there are written references to their construction in Kent and a probable excavated example in the earliest circuit of the fortifications of Hereford, an important crossing-point close to the Welsh border where a battle between Mercians and Welsh was fought in 760.

Bede felt that it might in certain circumstances be permissable for kings to reclaim land given to 'false' monasteries and put it to better use. Mercian kings certainly hoped to refurbish royal land holdings in this way and, in particular, expected to be able to take over royal monastic foundations of the kings of Kent and the Hwicce as a corollary of annexing their kingdoms. But they met stout resistance from the Archbishop of Canterbury and the Bishop of Worcester (the diocesan of the Hwicce) who argued that once land had been granted for ecclesiastical purposes it could not be reclaimed by laymen and that to attempt to do so was a crime against God. The bishops and leading abbots of southern England met regularly throughout the eighth century, in councils convened by the archbishops of Canterbury and collectively began to assert church rights and to ensure conformity with the universal laws of the church. They may have been in part encouraged by similar activities in Francia that were a facet of the Carolingian renaissance. Anglo-Saxon churchmen, who worked under the protection of Frankish kings to convert Germanic peoples on the fringes of Francia with whom the Anglo-Saxons felt kinship, may have helped the Anglo-Saxon church to keep in touch with Continental developments. It was the West Saxon Boniface, Archbishop of Mainz, who wrote to King Æthelbald to rebuke him for unjust demands on the church and an unhealthy interest in nuns. Some things were better said by a man several hundred miles from the seat of Mercian power.

Offa hoped to circumvent the southern bishops by establishing his own direct contact with the Pope – generous donations of alms seem to have helped smooth the way. By such means he was able to acquire a special papal privilege for churches that he and his wife acquired or founded, all of which were dedicated to St Peter. Two of their new foundations were at St Albans and Bedford – the latter was where Offa was to be buried. In order to outmanoeuvre the Archbishop of Canterbury, Offa received papal support for turning the Mercian episcopal see of Lichfield into an archbishopric in 787. Offa may have won this first round, but his successor Coenwulf had to agree to the disbanding of the new archbishopric, and his widow Cynethryth had a long, hard battle with the Archbishop of Canterbury to try to retain control of some of the foundations which the papal privilege had been designed to protect.

One of the major reasons why Offa seems to have desired his own archbishopric was so that he could have his son Ecgfrith consecrated as king, a ceremony which the Archbishop of Canterbury had presumably refused to perform. Offa hoped that by having Ecgfrith crowned as king during his lifetime he could avoid a dispute over the succession after his death. What Offa did not foresee was that his son would survive him by only a few months. Ecgfrith's untimely death was interpreted by one contemporary as divine judgement for the number of rivals Offa had had killed to try to ensure the continuation of his own royal line; the next king, Coenwulf, was at best an extremely distant relative. Offa may also have hoped to make Ecgfrith's position more secure by enhancing the position of his mother Cynethryth. She is the only Anglo-Saxon queen in whose name a coinage is known to have been issued and is named jointly with Offa in their papal privilege.

Ecgfrith is the first Anglo-Saxon prince known to have been consecrated as king, and Offa almost certainly borrowed the idea from the Carolingian royal house in Francia, whose king Pepin had introduced the rite to make up for his lack of royal blood when he deposed the last Merovingian ruler in 751. Francia continued to be as important an influence on the Anglo-Saxon royal courts as it had been in the seventh century, and no one was more influential than Offa's contemporary Charles the Great, or Charlemagne. Offa and Charlemagne were in diplomatic contact, and a marriage between their children was apparently mooted at one time. But Offa had reason to be wary of Charlemagne who was not adverse to interfering in the affairs of neighbouring kingdoms. The Frankish court sheltered at various times exiled princes and nobles from Mercia, Wessex and Northumbria; when King Eardwulf returned to his native Northumbria from Frankish exile in 808, he was escorted by Frankish envoys. Charlemagne was kept informed on Anglo-Saxon affairs by his Northumbrian adviser Alcuin who had been invited from York to assist at Charlemagne's palace school because of his skills in teaching, which ultimately drew upon methods used by Bede. From the security of Charlemagne's court Alcuin sent letters of advice to Anglo-Saxon England, and especially to his native Northumbria whose churchmen and rulers were rebuked for poor observance of Christian standards. He was rather more admiring of Offa, at least while he was alive; it was Alcuin who saw divine vengeance in the early death of Ecgfrith.

Francia was also an important trading partner of the Anglo-Saxons. Trade is a major concern in a surviving letter from Charlemagne to Offa in which he promises that 'black stones' (perhaps millstones) will be available in the desired size providing English cloaks return to their former length. The letter also refers to the protection kings provided for merchants which was a concern of the seventh-century Anglo-Saxon lawcodes too. By the eighth century most of the major kingdoms had specialist trading enclaves or *wics* in which merchants could transact their business under the supervision of royal officials who would also collect tolls and other payments on behalf of their royal masters; the financial advantages no doubt help to explain the royal interest. Ipswich, Hamwic (Southampton), London and York were all flourishing *wics* during the eighth century and excavation has revealed some of the goods which they imported, such as pottery, and the industries, such as bone comb-making and metalworking, which took place within them. We can see that the English *wics* belonged to a network of similar emporia found throughout the North Sea area, including Scandinavia. Small silver coins called *sceatta* were utilised throughout the region until Charlemagne reformed the coinage and introduced the larger silver penny which was adopted in England as well. Trade seems to have flourished in the eighth century, but unfortunately traders could bring raiders in their wake.

FIVE

Vikings

The Anglo-Saxon provinces were used to warfare
between themselves and with their Celtic
neighbours, but seem to have been taken completely
by surprise when their eastern and southern coasts
suffered seaborne raids from the end of the eighth
century: 'Lo, it is nearly 350 years that we and our
fathers have inhabited this most lovely land, and
never before has such terror appeared in Britain as
we have now suffered from a pagan race, nor was it
thought that such an inroad from the sea could be
made.' So wrote Alcuin after a raid on the
monastery of Lindisfarne in 793 which appears to
have particularly shocked the Anglo-Saxons, as this
was one of the oldest monastic communities and the
burial place of St Cuthbert, the patron saint of
Northumbria. Ironically, the Anglo-Saxons were
suffering from another Germanic people the type of
attacks they had inflicted on the British in the fifth

century, and were reacting with rather similar expressions of outrage. Like Gildas, Alcuin could not resist the opportunity of pointing out to clerics and to royal courts that the attacks could be seen as God's punishment for moral backsliding. 'Consider carefully, brothers, and examine diligently, lest perchance this unaccustomed and unheard-of evil was merited by some unheard-of evil practice', he advised the Lindisfarne community.

These aggressors came from Scandinavia and are popularly known today as the Vikings, though that was not a term regularly used by their contemporaries. People from Denmark and Norway were among those who had settled in Britain in the fifth century, though their Anglo-Saxon descendants may, at best, have been only dimly aware of this link. Anglo-Saxons may not have expected raiders to come across the North Sea, but they were familiar with trading vessels coming from Scandinavia. Indeed, when a group of Norwegian raiders turned up off the coast of Dorset towards the end of the eighth century, the local royal official (a reeve) assumed that they had come to trade and tried to take them to Dorchester so that they could present their credentials. However, when they slew him and hurriedly made off, the West Saxons became aware that a new phase in Anglo-Scandinavian relations had begun.

These first raiders, who also attacked Lindisfarne, seem to have been Norwegians. They may well have begun as pirate raiders in the wake of more legitimate shipping, but from an early stage they seem to have been on the lookout for land on which to settle. The shortage of good farming land in Norway meant there was a pool of potential settlers should the right opportunity present itself. They were more interested in the Scottish Isles and Ireland – which were reached by a direct sailing route from Norway – than in England. The early English raids were opportunistic explorations from their Scottish and Irish bases and, although unfortunate for individual religious houses or coastal settlements, did not pose any major threat to internal stability. A potentially more serious threat to Wessex, when the raiders joined forces with the Cornish who wanted to resist incorporation by the West Saxons, was decisively dealt with by King Ecgbert at the battle of Hingston Down in 838. The Norwegians concentrated on colonising the Isle of Man, western Ireland and the islands and coasts of

Scotland, and spread from there to the newly discovered Faroes and Iceland. However, there would be some penetration of these Hiberno-Vikings into the north-west of Britain in the early tenth century.

For most of the ninth century the more serious threat to the Anglo-Saxon kingdoms came from the Danes. The Danish assaults on western Europe may have had their roots in political resistance to the Franks, who had upset the balance of power along the North Sea littoral when they annexed Frisia and Saxony and brought their borders up to those of Denmark. As Charlemagne's biographer Einhard observed, 'if the Franks are your friends then they are not your neighbours'. Danish aggression was at first directed at Frankish coastal targets and raids on England were less frequent, but probably a natural extension of this activity. The raids may have begun with the desire of Danish rulers to utilise attack as a form of defence to discourage Frankish conquest, but those carrying out the raids no doubt soon found them a profitable activity which required no further motivation. Their attacks were frequently on centres where wealth might be expected, including Hamwic (840) and Winchester

(860); the fleets became larger and more difficult for the Anglo-Saxons to counter as the 840s and 850s progressed. Nevertheless, the Anglo-Saxon provincial armies seem to have been large enough to see them off.

It is not clear how far the Anglo-Saxons were aware of the pressures which lay behind the Scandinavian assaults. Those such as Alcuin who offered any analysis were most struck by the fact that the raiders were pagan and were at their most indignant when the targets of their attacks were religious houses. Subsequently, King Alfred developed the idea of Christian Anglo-Saxons defending not only their homeland, but also their faith against pagan aggressors. The matter is debated, but there does not seem to be much hard evidence to support the notion that the Scandinavians who attacked England were motivated by a hatred of Christianity. Raids on Lindisfarne were opportunistic ones on wealthy, unguarded settlements. Nor is it true to say that the Vikings 'destroyed' religious houses; Lindisfarne may have been raided, but the fact that Alcuin was writing to its community urging it to mend its ways shows that it continued to exist; it was some years later that the decision was made to withdraw from the coast to a safer inland location. Anglo-Saxon rulers may have respected the holy vessels, treasures and monks, but were not above attacking a church if it became involved in politics. In 750 King Eadberht of Northumbria had arrested the Bishop of Lindisfarne, besieged his church and forcibly removed a political opponent who had claimed sanctuary. Scandinavian paganism may not have been of as much concern to laymen as it was to churchmen, who were constantly vigilant for Christian ceremonies being corrupted by remnants of non-Christian religious practices surviving among the Anglo-Saxons. One of Alcuin's complaints was that Scandinavian haircuts and beards had become fashionable in Northumbria in the late eighth century, suggesting a desire to emulate, rather than to shun.

A number of the Anglo-Saxon dynasties possibly originated with a warleader who used his wealth and military power to establish a kingdom, and some of the Scandinavian leaders who came to England seem to have had similar aspirations. It was the Scandinavians who came without the intention of leaving again who posed the greatest threat; the most serious of all came from the Great Army led by the sons of the legendary Ragnar Lothbrok ('Hairy Breeches'), which arrived in 866. This army seems to have been larger than any Scandinavian force which had come before and probably numbered several thousands. It was soon revealed as being too large for the army from any one Anglo-Saxon kingdom to defeat decisively. Its first major success was in Northumbria in 867 which was caught off guard while two rival kings disputed the throne. The Great Army defeated and killed both claimants and began to take charge of the province. Its ambitions were temporarily halted the following year when it moved on Nottingham, but on seeing the size of a joint Mercian and West Saxon army, decided to sue for peace. In 870 it was the turn of East Anglia, and its king Edmund was defeated and slain; he was buried and commemorated at what came to be known as Bury St Edmunds. In 871 the Great Army moved on Wessex; the sides were evenly matched and nine major engagements were fought in the year without either side winning an absolute advantage. At the height of the conflict King Æthelred died, but the West Saxons had anticipated such an eventuality and his brother Alfred was on hand to succeed immediately. He established a temporary peace with his Scandinavian opponents. In 874 they tried Mercia; they drove out its king and reached an accommodation with the remaining Mercian leaders.

At this stage some of the army decided to settle for what they had already won in Northumbria and Mercia, but the survivors under the command of Guthrum moved on the last-surviving Anglo-Saxon province – Wessex. They came close to success in 878 when they caught Alfred unawares while he was celebrating the New Year at Chippenham. However, he managed to escape to the Somerset levels where – at his lowest point, with Vikings overrunning parts of Wessex – the legendary cake-burning episode is supposed to have taken place. By the summer Alfred was in a position to rally his forces, and he decisively defeated Guthrum's army at Edington in Wiltshire. A more lasting peace was established, sealed by Guthrum's baptism, with Alfred as his sponsor, and his withdrawal to East Anglia as its king. The worst was now over for Wessex, though Alfred was not to know that. There was always the danger that further armies would cross from the Continent and make common cause with the Scandinavian armies in eastern England, as did indeed happen in 885 and in the 890s. But Alfred had used the intervening time wisely to ensure that any subsequent Viking arrivals would find Wessex an even more formidable opponent than before.

Alfred's preparations included a reorganisation of the rota of military service and a refurbishing of the West Saxon fleet with the aid of Frisian sailors, but most important of all was the ring of fortified sites or burhs that encircled Wessex. Alfred was not the first to use burhs against the Vikings. Offa had built some in Kent, and a few sites in Wessex, such as Wareham, seem to have been fortified before Alfred came to the throne. But Alfred seems to have greatly extended the system and introduced the idea of permanent garrisons which could be mobilised against a Viking army as soon as it appeared in the district. They were used to good effect in the attacks of the 890s. Royal resources and food rents could be stored in the burhs, thus denying any Viking raiders easy access to supplies and portable wealth. These were probably more important considerations than protecting the inhabitants of the local countryside. Nevertheless, the burden of building and garrisoning the burhs was laid on the surrounding estates, as is revealed in the document known as the *Burghal Hidage*.

The Great Army's military successes resulted in the settlement of Scandinavians, predominantly Danes, in much of the eastern half of England which is sometimes known from this time as the Danelaw. As with the Anglo-Saxon settlement some four hundred years earlier, there is much debate about the scale of settlement; whether it was restricted to the Great Army and its followers, or if more people subsequently migrated from Scandinavia to England in its wake. Not all the indicators point in the same direction. For instance, there have been very few finds of burials of pagan Scandinavian type in eastern England, and generally much less evidence for Scandinavian cultural forms than in the Norse colonies in the Isle of Man and some of the Scottish islands. The settlers seem to have readily converted to Christianity which would have made social intercourse and marriage with Anglo-Saxons much easier. Viking leaders were patrons of the archbishopric of York and the community of St Cuthbert from Lindisfarne. On the other hand, the scale of the Old Norse place-name evidence suggests substantial Scandinavian influence, though with considerable regional variation in its density. Some scholars suggest that Norse dialects may have continued to be spoken in the Danelaw up to the Norman Conquest, and there were influences from Old Norse on language and grammar used in eastern England which are still reflected in the English spoken today. But the language evidence need not necessarily mean large-scale settlement by Scandinavian peasants, as was once believed. Many of those who settled would have done so as landowners and so might have had an influence out of proportion to their numbers.

Certain differences in the development of eastern and western England reflect the results of Scandinavian settlement. In the east in order to accommodate the army veterans, large estates, which had belonged to the vanquished royal houses and some of the major religious houses associated with them, were split up into much smaller units. Some Scandinavians may have decided to sell up and move on; others had profits of war to spend on purchasing animals and both essential and non-essential commodities, such as good quality wheel-thrown pottery which quickly began to be produced on some scale in several different centres. The result was a fluid land market and an active economy which resulted in towns flourishing in eastern England before they did in the west. Towns like York and Lincoln probably benefited from a greater degree of Scandinavian trade, and contacts with the Norse colonies in Scotland and Ireland, but on the well-known 'Jorvik' site in York which was developed after the Viking settlement, there is little that is diagnostically Scandinavian. It may have been not so much the settlement of Scandinavians, but the opportunities created by the break-up of former regimes that was responsible for these economic developments.

In the early decades of the tenth century a distinctive Anglo-Scandinavian society developed in much of the Danelaw. Its leaders fostered styles that often combined elements of both cultures, to be seen, for instance, in the distinctive stone grave-monuments to be found in many parts of Yorkshire and adjoining northern counties. Their connections were more likely to be with other areas of Britain than with the Scandinavian homelands. Not long after the battle of Edington, a treaty was drawn up between Alfred and Guthrum establishing conditions for trade between the different communities they controlled. The social equivalence of different Scandinavian and Anglo-Saxon classes was established so that compensation could be offered if there were any unfortunate incidents; both sides were worried that their slaves might flee to the other. In East Anglia, Guthrum produced a coinage modelled on that of Alfred's on which he used his baptismal, Anglo-Saxon name – Athelstan. Links between east and west would become stronger still in the tenth century when the whole country was united under the rule of the West Saxon dynasty.

SIX

The Kingdom of England

The conquests of the Great Army had transformed the political map of the country, as can be seen from Map 2. By the late ninth century, the only one of the Anglo-Saxon kingdoms to have survived intact was the kingdom of Wessex, which consisted of all England south of the Thames and was ruled by King Alfred (871–99). Western Mercia also remained under Anglo-Saxon control, but its ruler Æthelred recognised the overlordship of King Alfred and had the title 'Lord of the Mercians'. Their alliance had been sealed in 886 when Alfred entrusted Æthelred with London, which had been recovered from Viking control and was a former Mercian centre. At about the same time Æthelred married Alfred's daughter Æthelflaed. Eastern England from the Tees to the Thames estuary was divided between disparate Danish leaders. York and East Anglia were ruled by kings, but in the East Midlands control lay with earls based in the Five Boroughs of Derby, Leicester, Lincoln, Nottingham and Stamford, with their attendant districts. North of the Tees, the remnant of the kingdom of Northumbria was divided between several ealdormen, of whom the most significant seems to have been Eadwulf of Bamburgh. The north-west of England was subject to settlement from the Norwegian colonies in the British Isles, with a major influx after 902 following the temporary expulsion of the Vikings from Dublin.

By the end of his reign King Alfred had utilised the advantage he had as the strongest, independent Anglo-Saxon ruler, to establish himself as more than just King of the West Saxons. The writings emanating from his court promoted him as 'King of the Anglo-Saxons', reflecting a new political order in which Saxons of the South and Angles of the Midlands were united under his leadership. Alfred's wife was a Mercian of royal descent, and prominent Mercians were to be found at Alfred's court, particularly among a group of scholars whom he recruited in the 880s to revive and reform ecclesiastical culture. One of these men, Plegmund, was created Archbishop of Canterbury in 890. Alfred's military strength also encouraged some of the smaller kingdoms of southern Wales to seek his protection, and one of the results was the recruitment to Alfred's palace school of the churchman Asser from St David's in the kingdom of Dyfed. Asser's *Life of King Alfred* was written in 893, and one of its main functions seems to have been to promote Alfred as a worthy overlord of the Welsh kingdoms.

Like other Anglo-Saxon rulers before him, Alfred looked to Francia for inspiration in developing his rulership. Frankish influence was aided by the recruitment of two Frankish scholars, Grimbald of Saint-Bertin and John the Old Saxon. Asser's biography of the king was influenced by Einhard's *Life of Charlemagne*, but it would also seem that Alfred consciously modelled some of his own actions as ruler on facets of Charlemagne's life as presented in his biography. One of the most prominent examples is his recruitment of a school of foreign scholars to spearhead a religious renaissance for both church and state. But not the least remarkable characteristic of Alfred was that he not only promoted a revival, but also played an active part in it himself and absorbed the models of Christian kingship which earlier Anglo-Saxon writers like Bede and Alcuin had urged upon their contemporary rulers. With the aid of his scholarly advisers, Alfred himself translated four works – the Psalms and books by Boethius, Orosius and Pope Gregory the Great – from Latin to Old English, and thus not only set an example for other laymen at his court to follow, but promoted the use of English as a scholarly language. Behind these works we can see a promotion of the English as one church and people who had to strive under the leadership of Alfred to preserve their heritage from pagan attack. Such ideas underpinned the new political unity of the 'Anglo-Saxons'.

Alfred's successors went further and established control of a united England. Alfred's son Edward the Elder (899–924) and his daughter Æthelflaed – who became 'Lady of the Mercians' on the death of her husband in 911 and the only Anglo-Saxon woman known to have commanded an army – led a concerted campaign to bring the Danelaw under their control. In 910 a joint West Saxon/Mercian army decisively defeated the Danes of York at the battle of Tettenhall, and over the next eight years Edward and Æthelflaed systematically obtained the submission of East Anglia and the Danelaw, and extended the West Saxon system of burhs across the

Midlands in order to hold down the newly acquired areas. After Æthelflaed died in 918, Edward was able to add Mercia to the areas directly under his control. But it was not all undiluted success. The Danes of York were so weakened after the defeat at Tettenhall, that the way was left open for the Irish-Norse ruler Ragnald to take over the kingdom in 919.

Irish-Norse rulers, who often controlled a kingdom stretching from Dublin to York across the Irish Sea, became the major threat to the new kings of England. Edward's son Athelstan (924/5–39) had to face a major coalition of Norse, Scots and Britons of Strathclyde at the battle of Brunanburh in 937. It was led by Olaf Guthfrithson, King of Dublin, whom Athelstan had expelled from York in 927. On Athelstan's death Olaf was back and conquered Northumbria and the Five Boroughs, but by 944 Athelstan's half-brother and successor, King Edmund (939–46) had recovered the territory. In 948 Eric Bloodaxe became the last Scandinavian ruler of York and it was only after his expulsion in 954 that Northumbria was finally incorporated into the kingdom of England. The enlarged kingdom enabled Edmund's son Edgar 'the peacemaker'

(959–75) to be recognised as the most powerful king in Britain. His position was reinforced by a special consecration at Bath in 973 as *rex Britanniae*, and a symbolic event at Chester in the same year when eight rulers of non-Anglo-Saxon provinces of Britain acknowledged Edgar's overlordship by rowing him along the River Dee.

Symbolic unity had to be underpinned by structured government. The kings depended upon delegating control of various areas of the country to ealdormen who were recruited from the highest ranks of the nobility and were often related to the royal house. One prominent ealdormanic family was descended from Alfred's brother, King Æthelred I (865–71). The areas controlled by the ealdormen might be the equal in size of some of the former kingdoms. Ealdorman Athelstan was known as 'Half-King' because he controlled all of the eastern Danelaw between 943 and 957. Two of his brothers were ealdormen as well and between them the family controlled over half the country. These were the right-hand men on whom kings depended, and together with the bishops, leading members of the royal family and other prominent laymen formed the witan, or royal council, which the king would consult on key matters of policy. When a king died it was the witan which approved the accession of his successor.

The key element of local government was the shire. Ealdormen would control a grouping of these, but the day-to-day business of shire management was the responsibility of another important royal official, the shire reeve (later sheriff). Wessex had shires from the eighth century, and some of the kingdoms, such as Sussex and Kent, taken over by the West Saxons had been incorporated as shires. The West Saxon system was gradually spread to their newly acquired provinces to the north of the Thames, with most of the new shires taking their name from the borough from which they were administered, which in many cases was a fortified burh – Leicestershire, Northamptonshire and Nottinghamshire are all obvious examples. The chief men of the shire met twice a year in shire courts which not only considered legal matters, but provided an opportunity for the officials to convey a variety of royal announcements and demands.

For administrative purposes the shires were divided into hundreds, except in the Danelaw where districts known as wapentakes fulfilled a similar function. In the Midlands the subdivisions do seem to have consisted of about a hundred hides of land, and these units may have been established when the area was shired. In Wessex the 'hundreds' were much more irregular in size and may have been of much older origin. The hundred was a convenient medium through which royal payments could be collected and public services imposed, and controlled local law and order through the hundred court, which was convened by the shire reeve every four weeks.

Control was further aided by the grouping of the freemen of the hundred into smaller units known as frankpledges or tithings, often corresponding to settlements, whose members were responsible for each other's good behaviour and might be fined for any misdemeanours within the group. Every individual's responsibility was reinforced by an oath of loyalty to the king, taken by all freemen over the age of twelve, which included the need to prevent crime and bring the guilty to justice. Crime was no longer a matter of concern primarily to the local community, but – under the influence of Carolingian legislation – an offence against the state, thus justifying the intervention of royal officials and the payment of part of the fines to the crown. There are more frequent references to prisons, and to death or mutilation as the punishment for offences from the tenth century onwards, and execution cemeteries have been identified that were set apart from the burial grounds of the rest of the community.

The shire and hundred system was the cornerstone of royal control and supervision. Its effectiveness can be demonstrated through the study of the later Saxon coinage. In 973 King Edgar carried out a major reform of the silver coinage which from this time was to be uniform throughout the whole country and carry the royal portrait with the title *rex Anglorum*. The coinage was to be renewed every six to seven years, and only coinage of the current issue would be acceptable for royal payments or transactions supervised by royal officials. The dies were sent out to the provincial moneyers from Winchester, and people had to travel to their nearest mint centre and exchange their old coins for new – and pay for the privilege. Finds from hoards show that these injunctions were obeyed. They generally contain only coins of the current issue, though these are likely to come from a wide variety of mints, a testimony to the high degree of commercial activity in the newly unified England.

The country was not only unified under one king, but united under one church – indeed, church unity had preceded the political. There had undoubtedly been some disruption to the church in the upheavals of the later ninth century, especially in eastern England where some bishoprics and major churches had disappeared altogether, their lands probably taken by Scandinavian settlers. The imposition of the hundred system may have involved some revitalisation of local parochial provision as there is some evidence for the promotion of one minster church per hundred. But the movement which received most royal support at the end of the tenth century was the reintroduction of Benedictine monasticism. There had been few, if any, true monasteries left by the end of the ninth century. The disappearance of provincial royal houses had been critical for many of them. With loss of their patrons, the bulk of their lands were likely to be claimed by local bishops, Scandinavian settlers or victorious West Saxon kings, leaving a small nucleus of priests to provide pastoral care. In the reign of Edgar, Bishop Æthelwold of Winchester, supported by Archbishop Dunstan and Bishop Oswald of Worcester, initiated a bold plan to restore some of the monasteries of the monastic Golden Age of the seventh and early eighth centuries. King Edgar restored former monastic estates taken over by the crown and compelled others to do the same. He was rewarded by prayers on his behalf in all the new foundations and the underpinning of royal power by ecclesiastical rhetoric. England once again had centres of learning and the ecclesiastical arts which could rival those of Europe, and the monastic movement of England had been stimulated by similar European developments.

However, ecclesiastical provision was not uniform throughout the country and it is one of the areas in which can be traced marked regional differences in spite of the tendencies towards uniformity. In Wessex from 909 each of the shires, except Surrey, had its own bishopric, but the rest of the country was not served nearly as generously; for instance, Dorchester-on-Thames was the only see for what had been eastern Mercia and ran from the Thames to the Humber. All the nunneries founded and patronised by the royal house in the tenth century were in Wessex, and kings, in so far as we can trace their itineraries, seem to have spent most of their time south of the Thames. The western and northern extremities were not fully integrated with the rest of the country. There were no towns, and therefore no mints, in Cornwall or north of York, and the culture and systems of local government in these areas preserved older structures. Although new laws of the kings of England were imposed throughout the country, for certain matters local custom was still important and three major subdivisions were recognised where West Saxon, Mercian and Danish law prevailed. The regional distinctiveness of these formerly independent areas was reinforced by the ealdormanic system, and might surface at other times as well. In 957 the country had been divided between King Eadwig (955–9) and his brother Edgar who was styled King of the Mercians. The death of Eadwig in 959 allowed the country to be reunited, but it is an indication that a unified England was a recent and, in some ways, fragile creation which could fragment if placed under too much stress.

SEVEN

Dynastic Strife and Danish Conquest

When King Edgar died in 975, aged about thirty-two, he left two under-age sons by different mothers whose claims to rule were supported by rival factions among the nobility. The internal peace associated with Edgar's reign was shattered, but the potential for conflict between the political leaders had existed for some time. A series of short reigns by young kings, from the death of King Athelstan in 939, had entrenched the power of the major ealdormanic families and enhanced the rivalry between the two major groupings, the descendants of King Æthelred I and Athelstan 'Half-King' and his sons.

The leading ecclesiastical nobility had been drawn into rival camps as well. Archbishop Dunstan joined with ealdorman Æthelwine of East Anglia, son of the 'Half-King', to support the claims of Edgar's eldest surviving son Edward, while Bishop Æthelwold of Winchester was allied with ealdorman Ælfhere of Mercia in promoting those of Æthelred, son of Edgar by his third wife Ælfthryth. It was Edward who was crowned king in 975, but armed resistance continued. Both sides took the opportunity to reclaim lands which had been granted to the reformed monasteries. Neither Æthelwine nor Ælfhere were opposed to monastic reform as such and both were patrons of favoured houses, but it is evident that both objected to refounded monasteries within their ealdormanries to which they had had to surrender land and which impinged upon their jurisdictions. King Edgar may have deliberately hoped the reformed houses would help counter-balance the power of these major figures.

The potential civil war was averted by the murder of King Edward on 18 March 978 when he was visiting his half-brother and stepmother at Corfe in Dorset. Later sources made Ælfthryth the main instigator of the crime and she came to be portrayed as an archetypal wicked stepmother. Whatever the truth of the matter, the guilt for the crime can be laid with Æthelred's supporters, who stood to gain most from the murder. Æthelred was not crowned as king until the following year, and a period of delicate negotiations seems to have been necessary to achieve a reconciliation between the two factions, which was aided by the removal of Edward's body from Wareham to the important royal nunnery at Shaftesbury. Bishop Æthelwold probably played a significant role in smoothing matters over, and was a major influence during Æthelred's minority, which extended to 984. But the murder of a consecrated king was a serious matter and some contemporary sources suggest it sapped confidence in Æthelred's rule. Pressure mounted to have Edward recognised as a saint, and Æthelred attempted to turn the idea of a saintly kinsman to his advantage by supporting the translation of the body in 1001. Edward, king and martyr, was to be a major saint at Shaftesbury throughout the Middle Ages.

These events, and the possible weaknesses they revealed in the Anglo-Saxon system, would have been noted with interest at the Scandinavian courts. Although the Danish settlers seem to have been well integrated into the new England, the Norse colonies of the British Isles were independent and actively affected by events in the Norwegian homelands. The Earls of Orkney came from the family of the

Norwegian Earls of Møre; exiles from Norway might seek sanctuary in Britain and their activities were of concern to the Kings of Denmark who aimed to become rulers of Norway as well in the latter part of the tenth century. So it may not be a coincidence that Viking raiding began again early in the troubled reign of Æthelred.

The first raid recorded is an assault on Southampton in 980. As before, the first attacks were localised, though this time focused on southern England, and dealt with relatively easily; it is not clear where the first raiders came from or who their leaders were. But in 991 the Anglo-Saxons received an intimation that they had something rather more serious with which to contend when the veteran ealdorman Byrhtnoth was slain at the battle of Maldon in Essex, an event commemorated in the famous Old English poem of that name. The forces on this occasion were led by Olaf Tryggvason, a potential claimant to the Norwegian throne, and Swein Forkbeard (*c.* 987–1014), the newly appointed King of Denmark. Unlike those in the ninth century, these new raiding fleets were not led by Scandinavian leaders seeking new lands, but by rulers and claimants hoping to refill their coffers and strengthen their positions in the homelands.

King Æthelred has been much derided for his failure to deal more effectively with the Viking attacks. His epithet of 'Unready' might seem to epitomise this reputation, but is not recorded before the thirteenth century and its actual form is *Unræd* ('no counsel' or 'ill-advised counsel') – a play on his name which means 'noble counsel'. Much of our view of Æthelred stems from the account of his reign in the *Anglo-Saxon Chronicle* which was written after his death, when the English had been conquered by the Danes, and is permeated by criticism of his reign and a detailing of the shortcomings of the Anglo-Saxon responses to Viking raids. The last years of Æthelred's reign may indeed have been grim, but it is unlikely that the whole of his reign was overlain by the expectation of defeat. It should not be forgotten that Æthelred had one of the longest of all Anglo-Saxon reigns. He successfully resisted severe Viking attacks for many years, and a case can be made for his adoption of a series of initially successful strategies which invite parallels with the tactics of King Alfred.

Although there is no Æthelredan equivalent of the *Burghal Hidage*, excavations suggest that many of the Alfredian burhs were brought back into service in Æthelred's reign and were strengthened by the addition of stone defences. Some additional hill-forts seem to have been brought into use including Cissbury (Sussex) and South Cadbury (Somerset). The wills of Æthelred's reign suggest that the range of equipment which those in armed service had to provide was updated and improved; the myth that professional Vikings were countered by amateur Anglo-Saxon peasants should be dismissed.

Æthelred also used diplomatic measures to try to outmanoeuvre his enemies. With the aid of the Pope, he brokered an alliance with Normandy to prevent Norman ports being used by Danish fleets which was sealed by his marriage to Emma, sister of Duke Richard II of Normandy, in 1002. Æthelred also had some success in breaking up alliances between Norwegian princes and King Swein of Denmark. Olaf Tryggvason was persuaded in 994 to fight for the English instead of against them, and Æthelred may have encouraged and helped finance his claim to the Norwegian throne, which kept Swein distracted from English enterprises until Olaf was killed in 1000. Æthelred was similarly successful in turning round another Norwegian claimant, Olaf Haraldsson (St Olaf) in 1014.

One of the more controversial actions of Æthelred was the payment of large quantities of tribute (*gafol*) to buy peace from Viking armies when they could not be defeated outright. Such payments were a recognised feature of early medieval warfare; they are analogous to the tribute early Anglo-Saxon overlords collected and had been a feature of ninth-century Anglo-Viking warfare as well. Unusually the actual sums paid are recorded for Æthelred's reign and on the face of it appear astonishingly large, rising from £10,000 in 991 by stages to £48,000 in 1012. Some of the silver coins which formed a large part of the payments survive in hoards discovered in Scandinavia. In addition to these irregular payments, in 1012 Æthelred instigated a tax called heregeld (army tax) or Danegeld collectable from every hide of land in order to pay for Scandinavian mercenaries led by Thorkell the Tall whom he suborned from Swein's service. As a whole the country seems to have been able to afford such payments and the machinery of Anglo-Saxon government ensured that they were collected, but contemporary sources show that even wealthy churches had to sell land and suggest suffering among the poorer people who were obliged to contribute.

Tribute and geld payments may have added to the disillusionment with Æthelred's regime towards the end of his reign, but the real ire of the compiler of the *Anglo-Saxon Chronicle* was directed towards ineffective military leadership. Æthelred did not lead the Anglo-Saxon army himself; the church may have encouraged the idea that it was inappropriate for an anointed king to do so. In fact, the entire army rarely went into the field together; rather individual ealdormen raised armies as required from the localities under their control. It would appear that armies from different districts did not always co-operate as they should, and sometimes matters were not helped by feuds between different members of the nobility. In 1009, for instance, a large part of a newly assembled fleet of warships was lost in a quarrel between two Anglo-Saxon leaders. The *Chronicle* compiler criticised certain members of the nobility in particular, and it may be that Æthelred was sometimes 'ill-advised' in his choice of advisers, as his epithet suggests.

Perhaps mindful of his brother's fate, he seems to have been on the lookout for intrigue and several esrstwhile favourites fell spectacularly from favour. For example, in 1006 Æthelred had Ælfhelm – a prominent Mercian noble who had been created ealdorman of Northumbria – murdered by his new favourite Eadric Streona. The action seems to have permanently alienated Danelaw leaders, and Æthelred's trust in Eadric Streona was to be the undoing of the English royal house.

In assessing the conduct of the tenth-century Viking wars, it should not be overlooked that Æthelred had in Swein of Denmark a formidable and talented military opponent. Swein's final assault on England came after several years of intense activity in which much destruction had been wreaked and record large payments of tribute had been collected; on top of that the 1012 heregeld may have been to many the last straw. When Swein arrived in person in 1013 the different regions surrendered to him without further fighting, and Æthelred was forced to flee to Normandy. But when Swein died the following year, the English witan invited Æthelred back; significantly, he agreed to reform aspects of royal government to which they objected if they would serve him more loyally than before.

However, it was apparent by 1015 that the King did not have much longer to live; both Æthelred's eldest son, Edmund Ironside, and Swein's son, Cnut, began building power bases in England. It was at this point that Eadric Streona established his reputation for treachery. He at first supported Cnut, but then defected to Edmund when he became king following Æthelred's death on 23 April 1016. Eadric's treachery at the battle of Assandun in Essex in the same year caused Edmund's defeat. Edmund and Cnut agreed to divide the country between them, but before their agreement could be implemented Edmund died on 30 November and Cnut was able to get himself recognised King of all England.

Cnut and his new subjects were able to come to terms. A huge tribute was necessary to pay off the army in 1018, but Cnut agreed to rule according to the laws of King Edgar and proved an active legislator himself; his lawcodes were written by Archbishop Wulfstan of York who had also been the main figure behind Æthelred's legislation. The surviving Anglo-Saxon princes were exiled and some culling of leading nobles took place, including the despised Eadric Streona. Danish housecarls were settled in many of the shires to help ensure cooperation with the new regime, but there was no wholesale replacement of Anglo-Saxon by Danish nobility. Cnut relied on Englishmen as well as Scandinavians to control the country, and in particular he promoted two individuals whose families were to dominate the politics of the eleventh century – Godwine, who became Earl of Wessex, and Leofric, who was created Earl of Mercia. Cnut further emphasised his Anglo-Saxon links by marrying Æthelred's widow, Emma of Normandy, and was assiduous in patronising religious houses favoured by the house of Wessex.

But Cnut was more than just King of England. The death of his older brother Harold in 1018 enabled him to become King of Denmark, and subsequently he ruled parts of Norway and Sweden as well. He was recognised as a major ruler in Europe, and just before his death arranged the marriage of his daughter Gunnhild to Henry, son of the German emperor Conrad II. Cnut seemed set to establish an Anglo-Danish dynasty, but it was not to be. On his death in 1035, a situation similar to that on the death of King Edgar arose, with two sons by different mothers in contention for the throne. Cnut seems to have favoured Harthacnut, his son by Emma, to succeed him as King of England and Denmark, but as he was preoccupied with establishing himself in Scandinavia, Harold Harefoot – the son of Cnut and his first wife, Ælfgifu, the daughter of ealdorman Ælfhelm – was able to become first regent (1035–7) and then king (1037–40). Harthacnut (1040–2) was then able to assert his claim, and rapidly established his unpopularity through imposing high taxation. Another of his acts during his brief reign was to invite his half-brother Edward, Emma's son by King Æthelred, back to England. When Harthacnut collapsed and died while drinking at a wedding in Lambeth on 8 June 1042, Edward was able to return England to the rule of the house of Wessex, but the clock could not be entirely turned back to the way it had been before twenty-six years of Danish rule had intervened.

EIGHT

From Anglo-Saxon to Norman England

In the nineteenth century the Norman Conquest was seen as a crucial turning point in British history, thus ensuring that 1066 is one of the few dates known still to every schoolchild. The advent of the Normans was traumatic, and in many cases fatal, to the Anglo-Saxon ruling elite, but most historians today do not see it as an event which put the country on a new course of development. Many of the features thought of as 'medieval', such as villages and parish churches, are now known to have originated within the Anglo-Saxon period. Although probably no one in 1042 would have predicted that some twenty-four years later William of Normandy would be crowned King of England, it is possible to see how the seeds of that victory had been laid during the events of the reigns of Æthelred and Cnut.

It was Æthelred's desire to prevent Scandinavian fleets from using Norman ports that had led to the alliance between England and Normandy which was sealed by his marriage to Emma. During Emma's second marriage to Cnut, her sons by Æthelred, Edward and Alfred, had been sheltered at the Normandy court, and so it was natural that when Edward became king in 1042 his entourage included some Normans and other French speakers, and that Edward favoured aspects of the court culture he had observed there. Normandy was also one place where Edward could look for some support to counteract the difficult political situation which he had inherited in England. Edward had become king not just with the help of Emma and Harthacnut, but also with that of Godwine, Earl of Wessex. Edward's indebtedness to Godwine manifested itself in his marriage to Godwine's daughter Edith and the eventual promotion of several of his sons to earldoms. Edward had limited room to manoeuvre, as is revealed by the events of 1051–2 where a situation seems to have been engineered which temporarily enabled him to exile Godwine and his sons and send Edith to a nunnery. But when the Godwines returned with several warships the following year, Edward had to capitulate and take them back.

Duke William's support seems to have been important during Edward's short-lived triumph – he is recorded as visiting England in 1051. William may not have been able to prevent the Godwines' return, but he did hold a young son and grandson of Godwine as hostages, presumably on behalf of Edward, and it was probably to secure their release that Harold Godwineson made his ill-fated trip to Normandy in 1065 during which his famous oath to the duke was given. There may be some truth to the Norman claim that Edward had nominated William as his heir, not least, as many historians have suggested, to spite the claims of his brother-in-law Harold Godwineson.

It was the lack of a suitable Anglo-Saxon heir that gave William the opportunity to launch a claim to the throne. Edward and Edith had no children. Edward's childlessness was later used as evidence for a vow of celibacy to support the canonisation which earned him the epithet 'Confessor', but may well have been due simply to infertility of either the King or Edith. Edward's lack of a son would not have been so serious if England's Danish rulers had not reduced the number of other potential Anglo-Saxon claimants. Æthelred had had six sons besides Edward, all named after previous kings of England. The only surviving full brother of Edmund Ironside, Eadwig, had died in suspicious circumstances in 1017, perhaps killed on Cnut's order. Edward's own full brother, Alfred, had died during an abortive invasion on behalf of Harthacnut in 1036. Rumour had it that Earl Godwine was responsible for his death and may have been another cause for antipathy between Edward and his over-mighty subject. The only one of Æthelred's sons to produce heirs was Edmund Ironside whose children were spirited into exile after his death in 1016. In 1057 Edmund's son Edward the Exile came to England and it may have been King Edward's intention to name him as his successor, but unfortunately he died the same year. His son Edgar the Ætheling was the only possible heir of the royal house in 1066, but as an untried minor was not in the best position to attract support. Neverthelesss, what Harold should have done in 1066 was to declare Edgar king and become his regent.

However, Cnut had shown that the rules could be changed, that it was possible for someone not of Anglo-Saxon royal blood to not only take the throne, but also, once crowned, to hold it with as much authority as any descendant of King Alfred. Therefore in 1066 a number of ambitious chancers, including William and Harold Godwineson, felt that they had an opportunity to become King of England. William had no more of a hereditary claim than Harold did; whatever Norman apologists might later try to argue, the fact that William's great-aunt Emma had been Queen of England (twice) did not give him any rights by descent to the English throne. King Harald Hardrada of Norway also produced a dubious claim, based on an agreement between his predecessor Magnus and Harthacnut. There was probably no more enthusiasm for the Norwegian's claims than for William's among the English, but his invasion in the north of England, with Harold Godwineson's disaffected brother Tostig, in 1066 had to be countered at the battle of Stamford Bridge, and the campaign seriously weakened King Harold's ability to deal with William's invading force shortly after. Another potential candidate was Swein Estrithson,

Cnut's nephew who was King of Denmark, but he was preoccupied with problems at home in 1066. However, the threat of a Danish invasion remained a real one and was feared by William after he became king.

These ambitious men were not attracted to England because it was some primitive backwater that could be conquered easily, but because it was a rich and well-organised country whose potential made a considerable gamble worthwhile. William seems to have hoped originally that, like Cnut, he could manage the country through a few close associates and some compliant Englishmen; it was only the scale of the continuing English opposition that resulted in a much more fundamental substitution of French-speaking aristocracy for Anglo-Saxon.

The Domesday Book survey of 1086 reveals the elimination of the major Anglo-Saxon and Danish families who had dominated previous reigns, but with many lesser Anglo-Saxon nobles (thegns) surviving as royal officials or tenants of Normans, often in rather reduced circumstances. More noble women survived than men, of course, and the wealthier widows and heiresses seem to have been sought as brides by new lords wishing to strengthen their claims to English estates. The Domesday Book is also testimony to the basic continuity of Anglo-Saxon institutions and settlements under Norman rule. The Anglo-Saxon infrastructure of hundreds and shire courts provided the framework through which the survey was carried out and it drew upon existing traditions of Anglo-Saxon record keeping. It can be compared, for instance, with a survey of landholding in Winchester made in 1057 which survives in part because it was incorporated in a later document, the so-called *Winton Domesday*.

Although there was considerable change among the landowning classes recorded in the Domesday Book, continuity of estates and their peasant inhabitants was assumed. It is no longer believed, as in the nineteenth century, that the Normans introduced quite new concepts of feudal land-ownership and manorialism into England, although there were differences between Anglo-Saxon and Norman practices. In Anglo-Saxon England a man might have two lords, one who owned the land on which he lived who could demand certain payments and services as a result, and another to whom he was commended and owed personal service. The Normans were not used to this distinction and saw the rights of landowners as paramount; their expectations may not have worked to the advantage of their non-noble, independent tenants, the Anglo-Saxon freemen. What the newcomers would have been familiar with were the basic features of the manorial system, under which many of the Anglo-Saxon dependent peasants already lived, and in which land was held in return for labour services on the lord's land (demesne).

The process of transforming the Anglo-Saxon countryside from a pattern of dispersed settlement to one with a much greater element of controlled, nucleated settlement had begun after the conversion period when kings had granted land, with rights over its inhabitants, to churches and nobles. It was a process which had not been completed by 1066, but was well under way especially in the West Midlands and parts of Wessex. The physical manifestation of these changes was the typical medieval village with planned settlement, arranged around a central street or green and surrounded by large open fields, typically three in the classical 'Midland' system, which were strip-farmed in rotation. Set apart from the village, but clearly dominating it and within its own enclosure, was the lord's manorial residence. The Normans brought with them the Continental fashion for castles, especially of the motte-and-bailey variety, but a number have been shown through excavation to be sited on top of Anglo-Saxon predecessors that included substantial earthwork defences and towered strong points.

Completing the ensemble, and often adjoining the manor house, was the estate church, the ancestor of the modern parish church. Many of the first estate churches had been of timber, but during the reign of Edward the Confessor a move towards rebuilding in stone began which continued after the Norman Conquest. Churches form the largest group of field monuments to survive from the Anglo-Saxon period, and the largest proportion of them date from the eleventh century. They are often described as Saxo-Norman, because they combine features of Anglo-Saxon and Romanesque architecture and it is often not clear on which side of the 1066 divide they should be placed. Romanesque architecture was one of the French fashions introduced by King Edward whose great rebuilding of Westminster Abbey was completed shortly before his death and in time to receive his body.

It is difficult to trace the exact processes behind the reordering of the Anglo-Saxon countryside that gave rise to these manorial villages, but a combination of the need to provide for a rising population and to meet growing demands of landowners, and royal taxation may provide the key. The change could have been in the interests of both lord and tenant, but the planned nature of the settlements suggests that landowners may have played a dominant role and the peasants may have lost some of their independence in the process. At the same time there was a trend towards settling slaves on the land, on rather similar terms to the dependent peasants, so that they could support themselves rather than being fed at their owner's expense. An acceleration of this process led to the disappearance of slavery after the Norman Conquest.

Life could clearly be hard for many Anglo-Saxon peasants. Archbishop Wulfstan in his 'Sermon of the Wolf to the English', written towards the end of King Æthelred's reign, describes the sad lot of many poor people when the heavy demands for tributes were added to years of poor harvest and cattle disease. In such circumstances previously independent farmers might have to surrender themselves and their families to a richer land-owner who would support them in return for perpetual service.

These hard times are reflected in the late Saxon cemetery excavated in the small settlement of Raunds in Northamptonshire; the population in the tenth and eleventh centuries consisted on average of around forty individuals, nineteen of whom would have been adults. Infant mortality was high, with one in five babies dying. Childhood was always a dangerous time and as a result the average life expectancy was only twenty years. Out of a total of seventy adult women buried in the cemetery, thirty had died by the ageof twenty-five and another twenty by the age of thirty-five.

Not all peasants lived under a manorial system, and even on manorial estates there might be independent peasant tenants. Allowance must also be made for regional variation. Geography meant that not all areas were suitable for exploitation by large-scale farming or a classic open-field system, and in these areas scattered settlement would remain the norm. The Danelaw was characterised by a greater number of free peasant farmers whose obligations to a local lord were limited. Nor was social mobility always downward in late Anglo-Saxon England. Among Wulfstan's concerns was a world where the natural order of things was inverted and English slaves were able to collude with Vikings to turn the tables on their former masters. Two professions which seem particularly to have offered avenues for advancement from non-noble to noble status were military service and trade.

The wealth of excavated evidence for late Saxon urban life makes it hard to credit that it was argued earlier this century that towns were introduced after the Norman Conquest. In fact, the Domesday Book suggests that England was among the most urbanised areas of Europe, and that as much as 10 per cent of the population lived in towns. The larger towns numbered several thousand people, perhaps as many as ten thousand in London, the largest of all. A wide variety of trades and industries were carried out within them; Anglo-Saxon Winchester had streets named after goldsmiths, parchment-makers, shield-makers and tanners among others. Many of the larger towns, like Winchester, were also major religious and royal centres, which boosted the influx of visitors from home and abroad and the diversity of their populations. In addition to the recognised boroughs in which the mints were located, the Domesday Book records other places as possessing markets or burgesses and many of these centres emerged as more significant towns in the post-Conquest centuries, especially as landlords sought new ways to increase the profits on their estates by developing their own boroughs.

Many Anglo-Saxons were employed in one way or another in the church. Church estates as such were not affected by tenurial changes after the Conquest, but as leading positions in the church became vacant, they went to Norman appointees. One of William's justifications of his invasion was that he was going to reform the Anglo-Saxon church, and he was able to obtain papal endorsement on this account. Among the Pope's concerns was Archbishop Stigand, a supporter of Harold Godwineson and a noted pluralist, shunned even by other Anglo-Saxon prelates. One of the main objections of the Pope, though, was that Stigand had not formally acknowledged his position, but had recognised one of his schismatic predecessors instead. The English church was little different from that of other areas of Europe and like all regions it had some of its own customs, but the Normans preferred those that they were used to in Normandy. These included adopting the Romanesque forms of architecture, and among the most lasting legacies of the Norman Conquest are the great churches and castles the newcomers built in the major Anglo-Saxon centres, which symbolise so well a veneer of Norman superiority over a base inherited and preserved from the Anglo-Saxon world.

Conclusion

It is natural to wonder how England would have developed if the Norman Conquest had not taken place. Would Harold Godwineson have succeeded in establishing a new Anglo-Saxon dynasty, or would England have fragmented into a number of smaller regions, each with its own ruling house? Would England have been spared the long and expensive wars in France, but instead been increasingly drawn into the political world of Scandinavia? Such speculations can be endless and no doubt many of the political events of the succeeding medieval centuries would have been different if the battle of Hastings had resulted in the death of William instead of Harold.

But perhaps the country's course of development would not have been so very different. One can point to various changes in personnel and the structures of government that were the result of Norman rule, but the basic infrastructure of the country was not affected. The pattern of settlements and local governmental boundaries had been established during the Anglo-Saxon centuries. French language and culture were adopted among the aristocracy, but never replaced the English language spoken by the bulk of the population. England had always been part of Europe, and the broader changes which occurred during the Anglo-Saxon centuries were mirrored on the Continent. Sometimes what we see are the results of common responses to early medieval trends, such as the dominance of military elites or a rising population, but there may also have been deliberate imitations of what had occurred in other provinces, especially France.

The introduction of Christianity and subsequent advances in the church and ecclesiastical culture are good examples of this responsiveness. Like all provincial churches, the Anglo-Saxon church had some of its own customs and idiosyncrasies which were the result of the country's particular history, but it had never been outside mainstream Continental fashions or unresponsive to broader ecclesiastical movements. So although there were dynastic and short-term consequences as a result of the Norman Conquest, it is more difficult to say which longer-term developments would or would not have occurred in any case. The Black Death and Gothic architecture, for instance, would have reached England whatever happened in 1066. Anglo-Saxon rulers may have lost political power, but the basic structures which came into being while they controlled the country were to prove a lasting legacy.

Further Reading

PRIMARY SOURCES IN TRANSLATION

Alexander, M. (ed. and tr.) *Beowulf* (Harmondsworth, Penguin Classics, 1995), but many other editions are available.

Douglas, D.C. and Greenaway, G.W., *English Historical Documents* (London, Eyre and Spottiswoode, vol. II, 1042–1189, 2nd edn 1981, reissued by Routledge, 1996); for extracts of sources concerning the reign of Edward the Confessor and the Norman Conquest.

Keynes, S. and Lapidge, M. (eds and trs), *Alfred the Great. Asser's Life of King Alfred and Other Contemporary Sources* (Harmondsworth, Penguin Classics, 1983).

McClure, J. and Collins, R. (eds and trs), *Bede: The Ecclesiastical History of the English People* (Oxford, Oxford University Press, 1994); also an edition by L. Sherley-Price, revised by R.E. Latham and D.H. Farmer (Harmondsworth, Penguin Classics, 1990).

Swanton, M. (ed. and tr.) *Anglo-Saxon Chronicle* (London, Dent, 1996).

Whitelock, D. (ed. and tr.) *English Historical Documents* (London, Eyre and Spottiswoode, vol. I, 500–1042, 2nd edn 1979, reissued by Routledge, 1996); comprehensive collection of pre-Conquest sources including *Anglo-Saxon Chronicle*, extracts from Bede, charters, laws, letters and some saints' lives.

Winterbottom, M. (ed. and tr.) *Gildas: The Ruin of Britain and Other Works* (Chichester, Phillimore, 1978).

SECONDARY LITERATURE

Abels, R., *Alfred the Great. War, Kingship and Culture in Anglo-Saxon England* (London, Longman, 1998); comprehensive study of Alfred's reign in the context of recent scholarship.

Barlow, F., *Edward the Confessor* (London, Eyre and Spottiswoode, 1970); detailed study of the reign and problems of the last Anglo-Saxon king.

Campbell, J., John, E. and Wormald, P., *The Anglo-Saxons* (Oxford, Phaidon, 1982, reissued London, Penguin, 1991); excellent introductory text with lavish illustrations of archaeological and artistic sources.

Carver, M., *Sutton Hoo: Burial Ground of Kings?* (London, British Museum Press, 1998); the latest results and theories on this key archaeological site.

Clarke, H. and Ambrosiani, B., *Towns in the Viking Age* (Leicester, Leicester University Press, 1991); a rather broader review of early medieval urbanism than the title might suggest.

Deanesley, M., *The Pre-Conquest Church in England* (London, A & C Black, 1961); currently the only overview of the church to cover the whole Anglo-Saxon period.

Gelling, M., *Signposts to the Past. Place-Names and the History of England* (London, Dent, 1978); introduction to the historical significance of place-name studies.

Higham, N.J., *The English Conquest: Gildas and Britain in the Fifth Century* (Manchester, Manchester University Press, 1994); *An English Empire: Bede and the Early Anglo-Saxon Kings* (Manchester, Manchester University Press, 1995); *The Convert Kings: Power and Religious Affiliation in Early Anglo-Saxon England* (Manchester, Manchester University Press, 1997); trilogy on the fifth to the seventh centuries; stimulating, but often controversial. For later period see *The Death of Anglo-Saxon England* (Stroud, Sutton, 1997) and *The Norman Conquest* (Stroud, Sutton, 1998).

Hill, D., *An Atlas of Anglo-Saxon England* (Oxford, Basil Blackwell, 1981); useful presentation of many different aspects and events of the Anglo-Saxon past through maps.

Hinton, D., *Archaeology, Economy and Society: England from the Fifth to the Fifteenth Century* (London, Seaby, 1990; reissued Routledge); cogent survey of archaeological evidence against the perspective of broader economic developments.

Hodges, R., *The Anglo-Saxon Achievement: Archaeology and the Beginnings of English Society* (London, Duckworth, 1989); history of the period from an archaeological perspective.

Kirby, D.P., *The Earliest English Kings* (London, Unwin Hyman, 1991); thorough discussion of political history up to the end of the ninth century.

Lapidge, M., Blair, J., Keynes, S. and Scragg, D. (eds), *The Blackwell Encyclopaedia of Anglo-Saxon England* (Oxford, Blackwell Publishers, 1999); comprehensive entries on all the chief people, places, topics and events of the period.

Lawson, M.K., *Cnut: the Danes in England in the Early Eleventh Century* (London, Longman, 1993), useful overview of Cnut as King of England.

Loyn, H., *Anglo-Saxon England and the Norman Conquest* (Harlow, Longman, 2nd edn 1991); concentrates on social and economic history; *The Governance of Anglo-Saxon England 500–1087* (London, Edward Arnold, 1984); provides a clear review of administrative history.

Mayr-Harting, H., *The Coming of Christianity to Anglo-Saxon England* (London, Batsford, 3rd edn 1991); excellent survey of all aspects of conversion and the early Anglo-Saxon church

Morris, R., *Churches in the Landscape* (London, Dent, 1989); fascinating survey of many different facets of early ecclesiastical development.

Richards, J., *English Heritage Book of Viking Age England* (London, Batsford, 1991); useful overview and discussion of impact of Viking wars and settlement.

Rollason, D., *Saints and Relics in Anglo-Saxon England* (Oxford, Basil Blackwell, 1989), full overview of this important aspect of early medieval religious life.

Sawyer, P., *The Age of the Vikings* (London, Edward Arnold, 2nd edn 1971); a controversial review of Viking raids when it first appeared in 1962 which has in many respects stood the test of time; also (ed.), *The Oxford Illustrated History of the Vikings* (Oxford, Oxford University Press, 1997); comprehensive collection of essays on many aspects of the Viking world.

Stafford, P., *Unification and Conquest: A Political and Social History of England in the Tenth and Eleventh Centuries* (London, Edward Arnold, 1989); best recent overview of the later Anglo-Saxon centuries.

Stenton, F.M., *Anglo-Saxon England* (Oxford, Oxford University Press, 3rd edn 1971); the classic study of the

Anglo-Saxon period first published in 1943, showing its age in places, but with excellent analysis of politics in particular.

Welch, M., *English Heritage Book of Anglo-Saxon England* (London, Batsford, 1992); good introduction to archaeology of the settlement period.

Williams, A., *The English and the Norman Conquest* (Woodbridge, Boydell Press, 1995); examines fate and role of the English in early Norman England.

Yorke, B.A.E., *Kings and Kingdoms of Early Anglo-Saxon England* (London, Seaby, 1990; reissued Routledge); traces history of individual kingdoms up to the ninth century.

Index